WhY?
Questions along life's journey

DARYL T SANDERS

ACKNOWLEDGEMENTS

My wife Barbara has been steadfast in her encouragement to me and for those around her to "go on with God." In 1977, we met Fred and Florence Parker from Bethesda Christian Church in Detroit, while visiting a church in Columbus, Ohio. We were struck by the confidence of Florence as she introduced herself to our group of friends gathered in the corridor after church. After greeting us, Fred and Florence did not rush out of church as visitors. They lingered because God had them on a mission. The Lord prompted Barbara to seek out Florence about a friend in Detroit in need of Jesus. Lengthy letters were exchanged. A deep friendship developed that has lasted for over thirty three years. We are so thankful that the Lord sent these bold evangelists into our lives to open doors of faith to "go on with God."

After some months, we visited Fred and Florence, at Bethesda Christian Church. It was a life changing church experience for us. Over the years, we came to know and love the Beall family who pioneered this work over seventy years ago. Now in their second and third generation of leading this grand church, Bethesda is standing strong as a testimony of the faithfulness of Jesus Christ. One of the things we learned through this outstanding ministry is that Jesus is alive in the Old Testament. The foundation teachings of this Church, written by Rev. Patricia Beall Gruits and Dr. James Lee Beall have been life-establishing truths. We are grateful to the faithfulness of their dedicated service and for the impact they have had on people throughout the world.

This book is a reflection of an open door to the "whole Gospel."

All rights reserved.

Copyright 2002 revised 2011

CONTENTS

	Acknowledgments	ii
1	Getting Started	Pg 1
2	The Blood	Pg 9
3	Red Sea- Trap?	Pg 16
4	Marah – Bitter Water	Pg 26
5	Elim – R & R	Pg 32
6	Wilderness of Sin	Pg 38
7	Rephidem – Again?	Pg 47
8	Mt. Sinai- Decision Time	Pg 56
9	Taberah- Again?	Pg 77
10	Hazeroth- Rebel	Pg 85
11	Kadesh- Ready?	Pg 96
12	God's Will?	Pg 109
13	Wilderness Agenda	Pg 116
14	Moses Final Teaching	Pg 124
15	Leadership Transition	Pg 133
16	Finally the Promise	Pg 139
	EPILOGUE	Pg 150

INTRODUCTION

The journey of Israel out of Egypt to the Promised Land has had direct impact on my life. As I carefully studied the children of Israel and their journey, it has given me an opportunity to apply their failures and successes to my own life. As a result of this study, I received a new understanding of God. How God thinks. How God relates to His people in every generation.

About twenty years ago, I read the following scripture with a new enthusiasm and excitement. I Corinthians 10:1-13 gives us two different perspectives: how the people looked at things and how God looked at things. Is it not true that each of us traveling along life's path have had questions along the way because we could not understand why certain things happened as they did?

Ironically, God's plan was for the children of Israel to pass twelve milestones (or steps) from Egypt to the land flowing with milk and honey. God's ideal plan was that in a little less than two years, the children of Israel would be ready to go in to the place of promise – yet they missed it.

Likewise, God has an ideal plan for our lives, and we are often faced with many roadblocks in life -- places hard to leave. How do we find the strength to do so? We come to many **"WhY's"** in the road – which way is the right way? **WhY** did this happen? **WhY** did this or that go wrong? **WhY** did they do that? If God had only done such and such, difficulty would not have happened. Or if only that person in authority had given Biblical counsel, then perhaps a tragedy could have been averted. Our struggles to understand God's ways seem to be never ending. We often collapse into a cycle of regret when things go wrong. God is divine. He has purpose for every place of affliction, sorrow or tragedy.

May this book be an encouragement when you face difficult places in life? And you will. May we continue to discover a new perspective of God? May we discover His way to look at life? Truly His way is the right way - the best way, and for that matter the only way.

1 CORINTHIANS 10: 1- 13

Moreover, brethren, I do not want you to be unaware that all our fathers were under the cloud, all passed through the sea, all were baptized into Moses in the cloud and in the sea, all ate the same spiritual food, and all drank the same spiritual drink. For they drank of that spiritual Rock that followed them, and that Rock was Christ. But with most of them God was not well pleased, for THEIR BODIES were scattered in the wilderness.

Now these things became our examples, *to the intent that we should not lust after evil things as they also lusted. And do not become idolaters as WERE some of them. As it is written, "THE PEOPLE SAT DOWN TO EAT AND DRINK, AND ROSE UP TO PLAY." Nor let us commit sexual immorality, as some of them did, and in one day twenty-three thousand fell; nor let us tempt Christ, as some of them also tempted, and were destroyed by serpents; nor complain, as some of them also complained, and were destroyed by the destroyer. Now all these things happened to them as examples, and they were written for our admonition, upon whom the ends of the ages have come.*

Therefore let him who thinks he stands take heed lest he fall. No temptation has overtaken you except such as is common to man; but God IS faithful, who will not allow you to be tempted beyond what you are able, but with the temptation will also make the way of escape, that you may be able to bear IT.

(Bold type authors emphasis, New King James Version used throughout)

www.blueletterbible.org is a great source for online scripture access.

CHAPTER ONE

STEP ONE

GETTING STARTED

Scripture Text: Exodus 1:11-15; 3:1-17; Hebrews 11

There are times in life when a decision to go forward seems like the right thing to do, but it is not. As we study the decisions facing the Pharaoh of Egypt and Moses and the Children of Israel and the circumstances of the great Exodus; we must consider the dynamics between the parties and the God of Israel's directions in the matter.

Egypt was an affluent nation. However, the national leaders were threatened by the prosperity of the "children of Israel." God's people were significantly ahead of the curve. "The Pharaoh and his counsel decided that they should be enslaved and all newborn males should be killed." It was believed that politically they needed to be brought under total control and domination.

But the midwives – the medical representatives of the time – would not cooperate with the edict. But the Pharaoh persisted. He ordered every Jewish male child killed after birth or the midwives would be put to death. This was a dark time for the nation of Israel living in Egypt.

The baby Moses was rescued from infanticide, and miraculously grew up in the house of the Pharaoh, nursed by of all women, his birth mother! Presumably she planted in his heart the promise of their heavenly Father -- one day the children of Israel would return to the "Promised Land."

Life went on for the Children of Israel as slaves. Their treatment was harsh, the working conditions were as you could expect for slaves. Their food allotments were limited and their health care was nonexistent.

At the age of forty, Moses looked in on the burdens of the people that were his brethren by birth. He discovered an Egyptian smiting one of his brethren. He looked around and saw no witnesses, so he killed the Egyptian and hid the body. The next day he came upon two of his brethren that were in a fight and he couldn't understand why. Didn't they have enough troubles without fighting with each other? As Moses tried to intervene, one challenged him, asking, "Who made you the prince and judge over me? Are you going to kill me as you killed the Egyptian?" Moses was suddenly filled with fear. Even though he grew up in the house of Pharaoh's daughter, it was known to the entire household that he had a special place in his heart for the Children of Israel. He "assumed" that he would be revered among his own people. When they so quickly turned on him he knew if word got back to Pharaoh he would be killed. He fled into the wilderness, and made a life for himself in the wilderness with a people that lived in tents for forty years.

Moses gave up on his dream; after all he had sensed that he would lead a great deliverance of his people back to the place of promise. Unfortunately, the people were not ready to go. Egypt was not ready to let them go, and evidently Moses was not ready to lead them – yet.

Most importantly, God was not ready to fulfill His promise. This had been one of those false starts in life. God had something planned, a key player sensed that plan, but not all of the necessary events were lined up. The premature start was damaging to Moses and his sense of well being. Obviously he had a heart for the people. He was willing to give up his advantage of fame and fortune to identify with his people. But God's chosen people were not ready to go because they did not hate their circumstances enough. They were still coping and hoping that things would get better. This is one of the great wonders of the human spirit. We have a tremendous capacity to adapt to adversity. We devise ways to survive. We make the best of bad situations. Fortunately, there is a mysterious place of "coming to the end of ourselves." Individually, it can take a long time to find that end. For a nation, it's even harder because some get there quicker than others, causing friction in the group during the process. God's prodding and pressures allowed this collective group to come to their end at the same time, for His ultimate purpose.

There is a Biblical expression, which says, "In the process of time." Always a poignant phrase, it reminds us that things are processed in us -- for us and around us. It takes time. It is a process.

During this forty-year period "called the process of time" Moses virtually lost his dream to lead. The Pharaoh of Egypt died and a new one took his place. The children of Israel were suffering more each day under the bondage of slavery. Finally, they cried out to God. And the God of mercy heard their cries and remembered His covenant with Abraham. His heart was moved on their behalf.

As this drama unfolds, we come to the miraculous scene of the "burning bush" where Moses has an encounter with a Holy God. God tells Moses everything is ready. Now is the time. But Moses had lost heart. He experienced death of the vision. Moses probably gave up on the return to the Promised Land in his lifetime, losing the desire to deliver his people. But in the subsequent conversation, God told Moses that He saw the affliction of His people and heard their cry. He told Moses that He "knew" their sorrows. This is a comforting scripture for us – God knows our sorrows. He is *always* aware of our trials. Then God presented a life changing challenge by telling Moses, "I would send you to Pharaoh." The stage is set for the deliverance of God's chosen people.

Moses had let the dream die, but God was about to resurrect it from the dead. Forty years earlier Moses had an undeniable stirring in his heart. Yet he had not been called - yet. Now, at this amazing bush burning encounter with a Holy God, the call comes loud and clear. Often a leader can know something, sense the direction, and yet the timing is off. At the age of eighty, Moses is being called. God had been waiting for a confluence of events. Evidently God was waiting for the people to recognize their desperate need of Him.

Throughout history there has been much confusion over the "waiting" time required for the confluence of events to take place. We learn, by this example, that a key to the timing is the right moment as evidenced by the "call to go" of God. The burning bush gives us a picture of the kick-off. Finally the journey is about to begin, and there are some last minute preparations to take place. Let's review the process:

1) The first key to this process takes place at the bush. God singles out Moses. He informs him that Moses will be sent to Pharaoh to lead the children out of Israel.

2) The second key is a revelation of God's delegated authority for the journey. The lines of authority needed to be established. Misunderstanding of authority has plagued God's people since the Garden of Eden. Moses' initial response is "Who am I?" God says He will be with him – not to worry. Moses' argument is "I tried that" – it doesn't work. Now comes one of the most important revelations of the Bible. What God says next gives us one of the subtle truths of Christianity. As we study this journey, we'll learn that the children of Israel traveled the next 40 years in conflict. The impact of this truth was missed time after time. It should make us realize that we, likewise, often miss this same truth. Moses asked, "Who should I say has sent me?" In other words, by whose authority do I have to get this job done? How does this authority get implemented to those required to submit and follow? A question for every leader God has chosen and called to service.

God's answer is, "Tell them 'I AM' sent you." To our western mind this might not seem like much. However, each time God reveals himself to His people in a new way, the nature that He reveals of Himself makes the way possible.

In Exodus 6:3, God says Abraham and Isaac and Jacob "only" knew Him by the name "God Almighty." In other words, they had a limited understanding of the God of heaven and earth. They understood enough to live for Him and believe in Him in their day. However, during this time in history, for the great deliverance to take place, both Moses and the people in general needed to know God on a different level. They needed to see a different facet of God. They needed to understand more characteristics of God. They needed to relate to the Lord in a different fashion and discover different methods to walk in that relationship. This is why it is very appropriate that the last book of the bible is named "Revelation." The more we know of God, the more all things are possible for us. At the end of this age, the church will need to know God in all His glory for the last great deliverance to take place. Death will be done away with, and the enemy will be cast in the lake of fire.

Without delving into all the ramifications of the name "I AM" suffice it to say that the Lord was revealing that the great unchangeable One was in charge. The God who is the same yesterday, today, and forever would be leading them out. The authority for the journey comes from heaven. Powerful Egypt could not keep God's people. The timing for deliverance belonged not to a man, but to God. The people did not take a vote to decide to get out of there.

God's people had evidently lost sight of their need for Him. Oh, He had been in their memory banks, but they had gone on with life such as it was. This was a great stronghold to be broken. Slavery of one people over another carries such a spirit of control that even when there is a legal release, a mutual focus lingers to generations. In the heart of God the timing was right and coincided with His promise to Abraham. He had told Abraham that the people would suffer and be in captivity four hundred years (Gen. 15:13). Therefore, the verification Moses sought was revelation of authority in the name of God called the "I AM." God also promised verification through some signs or miracles proving to the people that Moses was not some dreamer. He indeed was sent for the job of leadership.

The chain of command has always been a place of conflict for people everywhere. Who made you the boss? Who put you in charge? These questions were asked of Moses forty years earlier, so he knew they were coming again. Whenever change comes to people, the lines of authority need to be clearly defined. The western mindset says you can lead, as long as I agree to your methods and progress. When the going gets tough, leadership had better be well in place. Existing problems often come to the surface because there are always those in an organization that are eager to take over. The seeds of dissension are in every group.

The Bible says that there is no power but of God. The powers that be are ordained by or set up by, God (Rom.13:1). God, revealing himself as the great " I AM," had been using the oppressive authority of the slave masters to pressure the people to want to leave the land of Goshen that had been, up to the time of slavery, such a prosperous experience. But God had another place in mind for them, a land flowing with milk and honey. The nation of Israel would have split asunder had God tried to merely lead them out of this prosperous place. Most would have wanted to stay – why leave? Since God had prospered them in Egypt why not let them stay there so they might prosper again? But God had a better place He wanted them to dwell in. He wanted them in their own land; He did not want the Egyptians taking credit for their prosperity. Remember Abraham turned down gifts from the King of Sodom so that he could not claim that he had made Abraham prosperous.

After a significant false start, which sometimes can be a factor in preparations of a people, the first step of deliverance was now established. The people finally had enough. They come to the place of crying out in unity to God for help. God heard their cry. God called Moses to provide primary human leadership. God released authority in His Name of "I AM" that enabled human leadership to operate. God initiated the timing by saying, "now is the time." Aaron was also called by God to provide support to Moses; thus another element of human leadership was in place. God made the promise of confirmation of released authority to Moses so that any opposition could be dealt with. God gave the direction and method of confronting Pharaoh to Moses. *These elements of call and release of authority are the same for us today.* It is God and Him alone who verifies those called to leadership and when the time is right to go. Without these establishments don't move.

The old adage, "God may tarry, but He is never late," holds great wisdom. It behooves us to move slowly, waiting for the Lord to push us rather than us push Him.

We are better off waiting. This is not an excuse to procrastinate, but rather, carefully making sure that God has made the call. He will release the timing and authority to move us forward. There was nothing but Moses' own dream and heart moving him at age forty. But at eighty, it was God doing the moving. The burning bush verified God's timing and calling. God certainly knows how to get our attention. God knows when to get the ball rolling. Many of God's leaders have been dreamers - people that are able to see that anything is possible with God. Visionaries can see the end and they don't worry about hindrances along the way.

Moses had to be prepared to lead. He could not depend on his own power to lead the way. The people had to be prepared, including getting to a place to want to leave. God had to be prepared. As strange as that sounds, God had to be allowed to decide the start date. The fulfillment of His word was in His hands and in His time.

SCRIPTURES FOR THIS CHAPTER

Exodus 1:8-17 Now there arose a new king over Egypt, who did not know Joseph. And he said to his people, "Look, the people of the children of Israel ARE more and mightier than we; come, let us deal shrewdly with them, lest they multiply, and it happen, in the event of war, that they also join our enemies and fight against us, and SO go up out of the land." Therefore they set taskmasters over them to afflict them with their burdens. And they built for Pharaoh supply cities, Pithom and Raamses. But the more they afflicted them, the more they multiplied and grew. And they were in dread of the children of Israel. So the Egyptians made the children of Israel serve with rigor. And they made their lives bitter with hard bondage—in mortar, in brick, and in all manner of service in the field. All their service in which they made them serve WAS with rigor.

Then the king of Egypt spoke to the Hebrew midwives, of whom the name of one WAS Shiphrah and the name of the other Puah; and he said, "When you do the duties of a midwife for the Hebrew women, and see THEM on the birth stools, if it IS a son, then you shall kill him; but if it IS a daughter, then she shall live." But the midwives feared God, and did not do as the king of Egypt commanded them, but saved the male children alive.

Exodus 1:1-17 Now Moses was tending the flock of Jethro his father-in-law, the priest of Midian. And he led the flock to the back of the desert, and came to Horeb, the mountain of God. And the Angel of the LORD appeared to him in a flame of fire from the midst of a bush. So he looked, and behold, the bush was burning with fire, but the bush WAS not consumed. Then Moses said, "I will now turn aside and see this great sight, why the bush does not burn."

So when the LORD saw that he turned aside to look, God called to him from the midst of the bush and said, "Moses, Moses!"

And he said, "Here I am."

Then He said, "Do not draw near this place. Take your sandals off your feet, for the place where you stand IS holy ground." Moreover He said, "I AM the God of your father—the God of Abraham, the God of Isaac, and the God of Jacob." And Moses hid his face, for he was afraid to look upon God.

And the LORD said: "I have surely seen the oppression of My people who ARE in Egypt, and have heard their cry because of their taskmasters, for I know their sorrows. So I have come down to deliver them out of the hand of the Egyptians, and to bring them up from that land to a good and large land, to a land flowing with milk and honey, to the place of the Canaanites and the Hittites and the Amorites and the Perizzites and the Hivites and the Jebusites. Now therefore, behold, the cry of the children of Israel has come to Me, and I have also seen the oppression with which the Egyptians oppress them. Come now, therefore, and I will send you to Pharaoh that you may bring My people, the children of Israel, out of Egypt."

But Moses said to God, "Who AM I that I should go to Pharaoh, and that I should bring the children of Israel out of Egypt?"

So He said, "I will certainly be with you. And this SHALL BE a sign to you that I have sent you: When you have brought the people out of Egypt, you shall serve God on this mountain."

Then Moses said to God, "Indeed, WHEN I come to the children of Israel and say to them, 'The God of your fathers has sent me to you,' and they say to me, 'What IS His name?' what shall I say to them?"

And God said to Moses, "I AM WHO I AM." And He said, "Thus you shall say to the children of Israel, 'I AM has sent me to you.' " Moreover God said to Moses, "Thus you shall say to the children of Israel: 'The LORD God of your fathers, the God of Abraham, the God of Isaac, and the God of Jacob, has sent me to you. This IS My name forever, and this IS My memorial to all generations.' Go and gather the elders of Israel together, and say to them, 'The LORD God of your fathers, the God of Abraham, of Isaac, and of Jacob, appeared to me, saying, "I have surely visited you and SEEN what is done to you in Egypt; and I have said I will bring you up out of the affliction of Egypt to the land of the Canaanites and the Hittites and the Amorites and the Perizzites and the Hivites and the Jebusites, to a land flowing with milk and honey."

Hebrews 11:1-3 Now faith is the substance of things hoped for, the evidence of things not seen. For by it the elders obtained a GOOD testimony. By faith we understand that the worlds were framed by the word of God, so that the things which are seen were not made of things which are visible.

Hebrews 11:23-29 By faith Moses, when he was born, was hidden three months by his parents, because they saw HE WAS a beautiful child; and they were not afraid of the king's command.

By faith Moses, when he became of age, refused to be called the son of Pharaoh's daughter, choosing rather to suffer affliction with the people of God than to enjoy the passing pleasures of sin, esteeming the reproach of Christ greater riches than the treasures in Egypt; for he looked to the reward.

By faith he forsook Egypt, not fearing the wrath of the king; for he endured as seeing Him who is invisible. By faith he kept the Passover and the sprinkling of blood, lest he who destroyed the firstborn should touch them.

By faith they passed through the Red Sea as by dry LAND, WHEREAS the Egyptians, attempting to do so, were drowned.

CHAPTER TWO

STEP 2

THE BLOOD

Scripture Text: Exodus 12: 13:1-16

With God's supernatural rod of authority, Moses had ten confrontations with Pharaoh and his mystics before release was finally granted. God assaulted the Egyptians with ten sensational plagues that reflected the false gods they worshiped. Finally, after the death of Pharaoh's son, he let God's people go.

As preparations were coming to an end, in Exodus 12 we see that the start date was established. In fact, God used this time to change the calendar because it was so significant of an event. He established this month to be the first month of the year. The official starting point was to begin with a significant event to mark this era for all times. God called for the people to be all packed and ready to go. Their last sanctioned act was to slay an unblemished lamb. The Lord instructed them to paint the door post of each home with the blood of that lamb. The death angel would then "pass over" their homes. Every home without blood would suffer the death of the firstborn, both human and animal.

The significance of pass over is obvious. Being set free takes the loss of blood of something innocent and precious. Egypt is a picture of our world. God has made a provision for our deliverance from its' corruptive enslavement. It takes innocent blood for our deliverance through the shed Blood of Christ, the Lamb of God. Our deliverance begins when we believe His precious Blood was shed for our sins. Our ever-present God has established the way out. It was the way out for the children of Israel. It is our way out of a life of sin and bondage. God's salvation was unveiled through the shedding of Blood to reveal Himself in this relevant way to us today.

There is power in the Blood. We must understand the significance of this power. First of all, the Lord could have merely over powered the Egyptians and gathered the children out. However, there was a spiritual bond that resulted from the slavery relationship between the people groups. Therefore, the shedding of blood could only satisfy a spiritual debt. This pattern had first been revealed in the Garden. When Adam and Eve sinned, their relationship with the Lord was broken. As a result, the Lord took the life of an animal and shed its blood. He did this to clothe them with the animal's skins because they were suddenly aware of their nakedness. This principle carried forth to the entire concept of offering systems the Lord established with His people. Blood became the requirement for the errors committed by people before the God of the Universe.

Blood is the currency of the Kingdom of God. Blood purifies, and the Lord was declaring His claim on the firstborn of all. There is undeniably a spiritual dimension to life that is often missed by us. This spiritual dimension includes sacrifice and blood in the physical realm that has influence in the spiritual realm. The Lord said that an innocent lamb had to be sacrificed and the blood of the lamb was to be painted on the doorpost of each home. This blood was a sign to the death angel that home should be "passed over." The lamb paid the price for the firstborn requirement of God on mankind. The picture of His "only begotten Son" is in view here. *The Lord wants the first of everything.* The Lord was requiring the release of His people, His firstborn, if you will. Since the Pharaoh was reluctant, the Lord required the first born of every Egyptian household both child and animal. This broke the physical and spiritual chains the Egyptians held over the children of Israel. The slave masters had a control over them, which had ramifications in the spiritual realm. The shedding of innocent blood was the only means to break that control.

Finally, after a major false start, forty years earlier, everything came together for the journey to move forward as a nation set apart. God's word was performed and His authority was released to authorize the deliverance. After the shedding of blood, two million or so people with cattle, gifts of gold and precious jewels, began a march unprecedented in history and not matched since. The march was not as escaping refugees but was a migration of over two million people and was organized, disciplined, with established lines of authority and communication. God Himself was leading, using a reluctant man as His representative with the nation.

11 WhY?

It should be noted that the New Testament tells us that God had hardened Pharaoh's heart. This means that the pressure on the people came at God's hand. It was God driving the people to a point of complete despair and ultimate surrender. They became desperate to leave. After a while the children of Israel had found some comfort in their slavery in Egypt. Why go back to some strange land promised to Abraham? A land filled with kingdoms and a people needing to be conquered in order to live. They had learned to cope with what the Egyptians allowed them to have. God has more for us in life than merely trying to live with what comes our way. The key question is what does He want? God's people had trouble leaving Egypt because even under the terrible circumstances of slavery, the known, as bad as it is, seems safer and more comforting than the unknown.

Therefore, we have a tendency to put up with less than God has planned for us. In fact, even in a place like America, we tend to accept living conditions as the test whether we are where <u>we</u> want to be. We marvel that some people can live in an abusive situation, when in fact their situation seems better to the victim than the alternative. Too often, for them, they feel like there is no way out and nowhere to go anyway. For any of us, the journey out of the life we know might appear more threatening, or difficult than just making the most of our life's circumstances.

This is why personal vision is so important. What has God planned for my life? What does God intend for me? Unfortunately all too often positive change does not happen until we finally get totally disgusted or dissatisfied with the present circumstances. We need to look up – to see beyond the present and set our heart on the ultimate plans of God for us. He has a master blue print for everyone.

In Egypt, the Pharaoh finally released the children of Israel and now their preparations were complete. The journey was to begin. God had set the start time. God appointed the "set man," or His appointed man to represent Him to lead the migration. The people accepted this chosen leader. He delivered them from the spirit of enslavement by calling for the shedding of blood. The *power* of control was legally broken in the spirit. *The recognition of the power equation in life is vital.* We are told in the New Testament, that through the shed blood of Christ we have been delivered from the *power* of sin and death. We may still sin, but the only power sin has over our life is the power we give it.

The second step of the journey began, and there was no turning back.

SCRIPTURES USED FOR THIS CHAPTER

EXODUS 12: Now the LORD spoke to Moses and Aaron in the land of Egypt, saying, "This month SHALL BE your beginning of months; it SHALL BE the first month of the year to you. Speak to all the congregation of Israel, saying: 'On the tenth of this month every man shall take for himself a lamb, according to the house of HIS father, a lamb for a household. And if the household is too small for the lamb, let him and his neighbor next to his house take IT according to the number of the persons; according to each man's need you shall make your count for the lamb. Your lamb shall be without blemish, a male of the first year. You may take IT from the sheep or from the goats. Now you shall keep it until the fourteenth day of the same month. Then the whole assembly of the congregation of Israel shall kill it at twilight. And they shall take SOME of the blood and put IT on the two doorposts and on the lintel of the houses where they eat it.

Then they shall eat the flesh on that night; roasted in fire, with unleavened bread AND with bitter HERBS they shall eat it. Do not eat it raw, nor boiled at all with water, but roasted in fire—its head with its legs and its entrails. You shall let none of it remain until morning, and what remains of it until morning you shall burn with fire. And thus you shall eat it: WITH a belt on your waist, your sandals on your feet, and your staff in your hand. So you shall eat it in haste. It IS the LORD's Passover.

'For I will pass through the land of Egypt on that night, and will strike all the firstborn in the land of Egypt, both man and beast; and against all the gods of Egypt I will execute judgment: I AM the LORD. Now the blood shall be a sign for you on the houses where you ARE. And when I see the blood, I will pass over you; and the plague shall not be on you to destroy YOU when I strike the land of Egypt.

'So this day shall be to you a memorial; and you shall keep it as a feast to the LORD throughout your generations. You shall keep it as a feast by an everlasting ordinance. Seven days you shall eat unleavened bread. On the first day you shall remove leaven from your houses. For whoever eats leavened bread from the first day until the seventh day, that person shall be cut off from Israel. On the first day THERE SHALL BE a holy convocation, and on the seventh day there shall be a holy convocation for you. No manner of work shall be done on them; but THAT which everyone must eat—that only may be prepared by you. So you shall observe THE FEAST OF Unleavened Bread, for on this same day I will have brought your armies out of the land of Egypt.

13 WhY?

Therefore you shall observe this day throughout your generations as an everlasting ordinance. In the first MONTH, on the fourteenth day of the month at evening, you shall eat unleavened bread, until the twenty-first day of the month at evening. For seven days no leaven shall be found in your houses, since whoever eats what is leavened, that same person shall be cut off from the congregation of Israel, whether HE IS a stranger or a native of the land. You shall eat nothing leavened; in all your dwellings you shall eat unleavened bread.' "

Then Moses called for all the elders of Israel and said to them, "Pick out and take lambs for yourselves according to your families, and kill the Passover LAMB. And you shall take a bunch of hyssop, dip IT in the blood that IS in the basin, and strike the lintel and the two doorposts with the blood that IS in the basin. And none of you shall go out of the door of his house until morning. For the LORD will pass through to strike the Egyptians; and when He sees the blood on the lintel and on the two doorposts, the LORD will pass over the door and not allow the destroyer to come into your houses to strike YOU. And you shall observe this thing as an ordinance for you and your sons forever. It will come to pass when you come to the land which the LORD will give you, just as He promised, that you shall keep this service. And it shall be, when your children say to you, 'What do you mean by this service?' that you shall say, 'It IS the Passover sacrifice of the LORD, who passed over the houses of the children of Israel in Egypt when He struck the Egyptians and delivered our households.' " So the people bowed their heads and worshiped. Then the children of Israel went away and did SO; just as the LORD had commanded Moses and Aaron, so they did.

<u>The Tenth Plague: Death of the Firstborn</u>

And it came to pass at midnight that the LORD struck all the firstborn in the land of Egypt, from the firstborn of Pharaoh who sat on his throne to the firstborn of the captive who WAS in the dungeon, and all the firstborn of livestock. So Pharaoh rose in the night, he, all his servants, and all the Egyptians; and there was a great cry in Egypt, for THERE WAS not a house where THERE WAS not one dead.

<u>The Exodus</u>

Then he called for Moses and Aaron by night, and said, "Rise, go out from among my people, both you and the children of Israel. And go, serve the LORD as you have said. Also take your flocks and your herds, as you have said, and be gone; and bless me also."

And the Egyptians urged the people, that they might send them out of the land in haste. For they said, "We SHALL all BE dead." So the people took their dough before it was leavened, having their kneading bowls bound up in their clothes on their shoulders. Now the children of Israel had done according to the word of Moses, and they had asked from the Egyptians articles of silver, articles of gold, and clothing. And the LORD had given the people favor in the sight of the Egyptians, so that they granted them WHAT THEY REQUESTED. Thus they plundered the Egyptians.

Then the children of Israel journeyed from Rameses to Succoth, about six hundred thousand men on foot, besides children. A mixed multitude went up with them also, and flocks and herds—a great deal of livestock. And they baked unleavened cakes of the dough which they had brought out of Egypt; for it was not leavened, because they were driven out of Egypt and could not wait, nor had they prepared provisions for themselves.

Now the sojourn of the children of Israel who lived in Egypt WAS four hundred and thirty years. And it came to pass at the end of the four hundred and thirty years—on that very same day—it came to pass that all the armies of the LORD went out from the land of Egypt. It IS a night of solemn observance to the LORD for bringing them out of the land of Egypt. This IS that night of the LORD, a solemn observance for all the children of Israel throughout their generations.

And the LORD said to Moses and Aaron, "This IS the ordinance of the Passover: No foreigner shall eat it. But every man's servant who is bought for money, when you have circumcised him, then he may eat it. A sojourner and a hired servant shall not eat it. In one house it shall be eaten; you shall not carry any of the flesh outside the house, nor shall you break one of its bones. All the congregation of Israel shall keep it. And when a stranger dwells with you AND WANTS to keep the Passover to the LORD, let all his males be circumcised, and then let him come near and keep it; and he shall be as a native of the land. For no uncircumcised person shall eat it. One law shall be for the native-born and for the stranger who dwells among you."

Thus all the children of Israel did; as the LORD commanded Moses and Aaron, so they did. And it came to pass, on that very same day, that the LORD brought the children of Israel out of the land of Egypt according to their armies.

EXODUS 13:1-18 Then the LORD spoke to Moses, saying, "Consecrate to Me all the firstborn, whatever opens the womb among the children of Israel, BOTH of man and beast; it is Mine."

15 WhY?

And Moses said to the people: "Remember this day in which you went out of Egypt, out of the house of bondage; for by strength of hand the LORD brought you out of this PLACE. No leavened bread shall be eaten. On this day you are going out, in the month Abib. And it shall be, when the LORD brings you into the land of the Canaanites and the Hittites and the Amorites and the Hivites and the Jebusites, which He swore to your fathers to give you, a land flowing with milk and honey, that you shall keep this service in this month. Seven days you shall eat unleavened bread, and on the seventh day THERE SHALL BE a feast to the LORD. Unleavened bread shall be eaten seven days. And no leavened bread shall be seen among you, nor shall leaven be seen among you in all your quarters. And you shall tell your son in that day, saying, 'THIS IS DONE because of what the LORD did for me when I came up from Egypt.' It shall be as a sign to you on your hand and as a memorial between your eyes, that the LORD's law may be in your mouth; for with a strong hand the LORD has brought you out of Egypt. You shall therefore keep this ordinance in its season from year to year.

"And it shall be, when the LORD brings you into the land of the Canaanites, as He swore to you and your fathers, and gives it to you, that you shall set apart to the LORD all that open the womb, that is, every firstborn that comes from an animal which you have; the males SHALL BE the LORD's. But every firstborn of a donkey you shall redeem with a lamb; and if you will not redeem IT, then you shall break its neck. And all the firstborn of man among your sons you shall redeem. So it shall be, when your son asks you in time to come, saying, 'What IS this?' that you shall say to him, 'By strength of hand the LORD brought us out of Egypt, out of the house of bondage. And it came to pass, when Pharaoh was stubborn about letting us go, that the LORD killed all the firstborn in the land of Egypt, both the firstborn of man and the firstborn of beast. Therefore I sacrifice to the LORD all males that open the womb, but all the firstborn of my sons I redeem.' It shall be as a sign on your hand and as frontlets between your eyes, for by strength of hand the LORD brought us out of Egypt."

The Wilderness Way

Then it came to pass, when Pharaoh had let the people go, that God did not lead them BY way of the land of the Philistines, although that WAS near; for God said, "Lest perhaps the people change their minds when they see war, and return to Egypt." So God led the people around BY way of the wilderness of the Red Sea. And the children of Israel went up in orderly ranks out of the land of Egypt.

CHAPTER THREE

STEP 3

RED SEA – TRAP?

Scripture Text: Exodus 13:19-15:21

As the journey goes forward, keep in mind that there are two distinct perspectives: **1)** God's perspective and, **2)** the people's perspective. God's plan and purpose is at work so consider what He is doing and how He is viewing things. The journey is deliberate by God, with Moses, and the people in their role of responding to whatever the journey brings their way. There are no surprises for God. He knew everything coming before it happened. This understanding has many ramifications as we review their entire journey. Likewise, the implications for us are the same as we begin our own journey in life. We often make things happen by sheer will power, talent and abilities. But the older one grows so grows the realization that our control over life is much less than previously thought in our carefree youth. If He knows and allows it, then there must be a purpose. God's purposes always end up for good. Often that is very hard for us to fathom because we remain content in the present.

Let's consider the ultimate plan of God for His people. He was taking an entire race that had a slave mentality from decades of bondage. He was going to re: train them to be a conquering people. This requires a massive paradigm shift. To accomplish this, God was going to put them into difficult situations of need that were intended to teach them to turn to God to meet their every need. Each of these places of need also revealed wounds of the heart that the Lord intended to heal when they were brought to the surface. In addition, He was going to reveal various aspects of His nature and how they could embrace His love for them. In this pilgrimage they needed to put their trust in Him in a way they had never trusted before. This is mankind's common journey in life.

In one of the most curious challenges of leadership, they encountered an apparent trap before they left Egypt. Think of the timing! Surely there was great excitement as men, women and children were in wonderment, traveling over two million strong. Everyone was marching by family group. Suddenly, someone looked over their shoulder and saw the Pharaoh and six hundred warriors on chariots in hot pursuit! Imagine the words of fear that spread through the entire camp like wild fire. What are they doing? They will kill us! **WhY** are we here? **WhY** didn't we stay where we were? **WhY** did Moses do this to us? **WhY** did God do this to us? Surely the questions did not stop there. This took place at the edge of the roaring Red Sea. They were between the proverbial rock and hard place. They couldn't go back – although many probably would have tried if the Pharaoh and his army had not been charging toward them. They couldn't go forward, as the Red Sea could not be crossed. From the human point of view, without God in the equation, there was no way out.

Coming to "apparently impossible" situations brings out accusations and blame in human nature. The people cried out to Moses. "Were there not enough graves in Egypt that you brought us here to die?" In that moment of panic they revised history – even though their history was only a few days old. They said to Moses, "we told you to let us alone and let us serve the Egyptians" -- hardly the case!

At this very dramatic **"whY"** in the road consider what happens. Moses' first declaration is **"fear not!"** Those words spoke right to the condition of the heart of the people. Their accusations came out of hearts of fear. They had lived for generations in fear. A slave is a fearful person. One of the primary tools of a slave owner is "the threat." There is a constant threat of punishment and death. There is the threat of less food, and more work. The first step on God's agenda was to minister to this engrained fear. In order to break free from a slave mentality we must learn to be free from fear. God, in His mercy, set up an immediate place of need that would bring fear to the forefront. Out of the shadows and right to the surface. Fear was the primary stronghold that the Lord was attempting to set His people free from. He led them to this conundrum from which there was "no way out." He had a clear purpose which was to set them free from fear. At the same time He was also revealing a new understanding of their relationship with Him.

Secondly, Moses said, **"stand still."** In other words, there is nothing for you to do in this situation. It was one of those times in life where human solutions had no answer. So stand still and see what God will do. Thirdly, he said, **"see the salvation of the Lord."** Salvation is more than a state of mind. Salvation is the visible breaking of the power of death. Life is something that can be seen. Moses was saying, on behalf of God, keep your eyes open. Watch what happens and don't ever forget it. This journey is under the auspices of the Lord. God fights for you and keeps you in peace. The Lord instructed Moses to tell the people to march forward toward the Red Sea. He told Moses to raise his staff over the Sea and divide it. We know the miracle. With the help of Hollywood, we can remember the picture of Charleton Heston standing on the edge of the Red Sea, lifting his staff, and shouting, "Stand and see the Salvation of the Lord." The Sea parted and a path opened up for the Children of Israel to cross.

Even more than that, they marched across on *dry* ground, and they safely arrived on the other side. As the entire Egyptian army followed the same route across the Red Sea, they watched in horror as God pulled the plug. The enemy drowned to every last one..

The people were filled with ecstatic joy -- dancing and celebrating the great victory. Israel rejoiced with songs of triumph. Suddenly they acknowledged the greatness and goodness of God. They rehearsed to one another that the Lord threw the enemy army in the sea. They suddenly realized that the Lord is a Man of War, and He was their salvation. They now understood that they could exalt Him; God had mercy, He was in fact leading them, and He would reign forever and ever. At the end of Exodus 14 and the early part of chapter15 everything was just great. Every family member was accounted for and they were safe on the "other side". The people saw that God was both with them and for them.

The salvation of the Lord is most wonderful. On our own we are lost in sin and death with no way out, so it is glorious to learn there is "The Way" out. However, studies show that in spite of the fact that American's live in a land blessed with opportunity – fear permeates our culture. In our land of prosperity, where the sky is the limit, fear of failure is a stronghold over our nation. It is incredible how many in their early twenties are afraid that they will not be able to provide. How many older citizens fear old age, sickness, and loss of income? How many in middle age have come up short of their dreams and expectations?

After the end of the first decade of the 21st century the economic outlook throughout the world looks bleak at best. Wars and rumors of wars are raging in all corners of the world. Hurricanes, floods, and devastating earthquakes around the world have created a sense of the world itself between a rock and a hard place in need of Salvation.

19 WhY?

The word of the Lord to this generation is the same as at the Red Sea: Fear not. Our lives are in His hands. We can trust Him and believe that He is leading us. When we come to the brick wall in life – fear not! When we can't see a way, it is time to look up. He is as involved with us as He was with the children of Israel. We each have a journey to take. When we come to that **"whY"** in the road, don't accuse God, our leaders, or for that matter, ourselves. It is time to believe.

Coming to a place of no way out is time to *rejoice. We come to difficult places so He can reveal what is in our hearts. And more importantly, we have the opportunity to see Him as never before. What He illuminates of himself will be all we need to get through the present dark tunnel.* So often we pray to *get out* of the situation when He intends to take us *through* the situation with a new revelation of His greatness. To God be the glory. Come to think of it, we have gotten through everything in the past, so we will in the present or for that matter the future – as long as we look to Him.

Sometimes we want to throw in the towel and go back. Instead, let's look up to the hills from whence comes our help. It is the Lord strong and mighty, He will lift us up. At the Red Sea, God had Moses declare that the battle is the Lord's. So often we feel the need to fight. But the battle is the Lord's. My friends, the children of Israel came to a trap in deed. *But, God* laid the trap. Had they come to the Red Sea with no one in pursuit surely many would have turned back. God knew they would give up because they could not see the way with their natural eyes. When we hit the brick wall we must remember to put on our spiritual glasses to see in the spiritual realm. When we run out of answers it is time to look for His answers. If God has led us to a certain place in time, we can conclude that He knows what He is doing.

If we are uncomfortable, we shouldn't think something must be wrong – a mistake has been made. Life is not always comfortable. Pressures and pain are a part of every life – rich or poor. Traps and gaps are a part of everyone's experience. Walls and **whYs** are a part of every journey. The Bible does say all things work together for good to those that love God and are called according to His purpose. We are to love God and trust Him, regardless how difficult a situation might seem. When it is all said and done, we will be able to look back and realize that it worked out for good. Life cannot be measured by how good it feels along the way. History has proven that extraordinary lives were the result of difficulties worked through for the best in the person and in history itself.

It is said that the first eight missionaries to go to Africa from Europe (not counting the Eunuch years earlier), lost their lives before they landed. Jim Elliot's martyred life has been for good. Stephen, the first great preaching evangelist, lost his life and it was for good. Why didn't God let the likes of Peter, Stephen and Paul live for another 200 years and get the job done? With how productive they were they would have evangelized the world. God will not have heroes and glory going to another. His plan for history includes you and me. God knows what He is doing. If He leads you into a trap, be alert and open your spiritual eyes and cooperate. God knows what He is doing. He always provides a way.

Whatever surfaces in my heart during times of feeling trapped is what God is attempting to minister to me about. Times of great distress allow me to cry out for help. God longs to deliver me from that which is most debilitating in my life. The children of Israel were trapped and the first emotion to surface was fear. The Lord ministered to that fear. God showed up. He said, "to stand still and see the salvation of the Lord." Not trying to hurt them, He was showing them how to be healed. His word is healing, if we receive it. Times of feeling trapped provide an opportunity for the Lord to set us free from long standing hurts and weaknesses.

We've become a "feed good" culture because bruised feelings are being elevated higher than the Lord. Christian counselors are trading the cross for the couch. By attempting to heal hurt or avoid hurt, we will miss **whY** God has brought pain to the surface. It surfaces that He might show us how to gain freedom from it. We are preoccupied with the origin of our pain. We fall into a trap by thinking that if we find the source or cause of pain, we can be healed. Never once did God identify the source of their fear, nor did He tie it directly to slavery, or how others mistreated them. He would not allow wrong feelings to be justified. As a child of God, it is not necessary to live with fear. If we can identify fear, God has brought it to the surface to free us from it. He never told the children of Israel to forgive the Egyptians! He never said, "I don't blame you for having fear," or "you poor things, no wonder you are fearful – all you've been through!"

On the contrary, He led them out of their homes and right into a trap. He needed to quickly deal with a debilitating stronghold of fear in the hearts of the people. There is no place in the scriptures to suggest that we need to return to those who wronged us to blame them for *our* wrong behavior. Neither does scripture support the theory that we wouldn't be a certain way if others had acted differently toward us or treated us better.

21 WhY?

The hope of God in our lives is greater than any previous failure. The source of our pain and confusion in life is irrelevant when compared to the power of God. Finding and dealing with the source is not scriptural. Rather, revealing the very existence of the hurt, as shown by my response, is the key to my deliverance. When fear, rejection, abandonment, bitterness, or any of life's debilitating hurts come to the surface, it is not time to commiserate or calculate how they all got started or who did it to me first. Rather, it is time to offer it to God and find His word of healing. It is time to come to grips with my responses when provoked by people who bring negative emotions out of me.

Joseph was a bitter young man in prison for almost ten years. After interpretation of the butler's dream, he told the butler not to forget him because Joseph did not belong in prison. Joseph complained of being mistreated by his family and Potiphar. He was bitter and resentful, and one could say justifiably so. Two verses later, it says the butler forgot him (Gen. 40:23 then Genesis 41:1). It says at the end of *two full years* in prison, the Pharaoh had a dream. Joseph was given a shave and a haircut and brought before Pharaoh to interpret a dream. Joseph was made the number two man in the nation, in charge of all the economy of Egypt.

As we continue in the story, Joseph was never ever reconciled to Potiphar. He never demanded an apology from his brothers for their mistreatment of him. In fact, in Genesis 45:5-8, Joseph says to his brothers, "don't be angry with yourselves that you sold me in slavery – it was God who actually did it!" They had trouble believing him. After their father died, they worried that Joseph would get retribution. They came and fell at his feet and offered themselves as his servants (as he saw in his dream as a youngster). But Joseph said, "You meant it for evil but God meant it for good." While the brothers came to grips with their wrong behavior, Joseph had found his freedom from bitterness and resentment. Joseph accepted that God was in charge of his journey. Regardless of whatever God allowed to happen, God also was making a way of redemption. In other words, God was going to use it to do what needed to be done, no matter how awful it seemed at the time.

The Church needs to better understand that God is involved more in our lives than we realize. The devil gets blamed for things that God allows for our good. Joseph's heart was somehow healed in those last two years of prison. He evidently needed a *third let down* in life to understand that God was working in this dreamer's life. He dreamed of greatness as a young man. Perhaps his pride and arrogance would have been in the way without his mistreatment and prison experience. Or it may have been a way God kept him pure before women while waiting on God's timing to raise him to the leadership he had dreamed about? Who knows whether he would have killed his brothers when they showed up for food if God did not deal with Joseph's bitter heart? We know that God's plan to provide for the nation of Israel was to send Joseph ahead for the nation of Israel.

God did not want the children of Israel to build the land of Canaan by themselves. They would have taken credit for it. It was His plan for them to leave the land that He promised, for four hundred years, as God had told Abraham. By allowing others to build and prosper the land, they would always give God credit for fulfilling His Promise. We don't know all the details of how these things work, but God surely does. We must trust and believe.

The Lord is ordering the steps of every one of us here on Earth. He has a plan that includes taking us from whatever state we're in to a new place that He has set aside. When we trust that everything will work together for good to those who love God, we will operate in genuine faith and have victory in this present life.

This trap was solely to bring to the surface those negative emotions and hurts so God could heal them. To conquer the Promised Land, God's people needed to be free from fear. So do you and I.

SCRIPTURES USED FOR THIS CHAPTER

EXODUS 13:19-22 And Moses took the bones of Joseph with him, for he had placed the children of Israel under solemn oath, saying, "God will surely visit you, and you shall carry up my bones from here with you."

So they took their journey from Succoth and camped in Etham at the edge of the wilderness. And the LORD went before them by day in a pillar of cloud to lead the way, and by night in a pillar of fire to give them light, so as to go by day and night. He did not take away the pillar of cloud by day or the pillar of fire by night FROM before the people.

EXODUS 14:1-31 Now the LORD spoke to Moses, saying: "Speak to the children of Israel, that they turn and camp before Pi Hahiroth, between Migdol and the sea, opposite Baal Zephon; you shall camp before it by the sea. For Pharaoh will say of the children of Israel, 'They ARE bewildered by the land; the wilderness has closed them in.' Then I will harden Pharaoh's heart, so that he will pursue them; and I will gain honor over Pharaoh and over all his army, that the Egyptians may know that I AM the LORD." And they did so.

23 WhY?

Now it was told the king of Egypt that the people had fled, and the heart of Pharaoh and his servants was turned against the people; and they said, "Why have we done this, that we have let Israel go from serving us?" So he made ready his chariot and took his people with him. Also, he took six hundred choice chariots, and all the chariots of Egypt with captains over every one of them. And the LORD hardened the heart of Pharaoh king of Egypt, and he pursued the children of Israel; and the children of Israel went out with boldness. So the Egyptians pursued them, all the horses AND chariots of Pharaoh, his horsemen and his army, and overtook them camping by the sea beside Pi Hahiroth, before Baal Zephon.

And when Pharaoh drew near, the children of Israel lifted their eyes, and behold, the Egyptians marched after them. So they were very afraid, and the children of Israel cried out to the LORD. Then they said to Moses, "Because THERE WERE no graves in Egypt, have you taken us away to die in the wilderness? Why have you so dealt with us, to bring us up out of Egypt? IS this not the word that we told you in Egypt, saying, 'Let us alone that we may serve the Egyptians'? For IT WOULD HAVE BEEN better for us to serve the Egyptians than that we should die in the wilderness."

And Moses said to the people, "Do not be afraid. Stand still, and see the salvation of the LORD, which He will accomplish for you today. For the Egyptians whom you see today, you shall see again no more forever. The LORD will fight for you, and you shall hold your peace."

And the LORD said to Moses, "Why do you cry to Me? Tell the children of Israel to go forward. But lift up your rod, and stretch out your hand over the sea and divide it. And the children of Israel shall go on dry GROUND through the midst of the sea. And I indeed will harden the hearts of the Egyptians, and they shall follow them. So I will gain honor over Pharaoh and over all his army, his chariots, and his horsemen. Then the Egyptians shall know that I AM the LORD, when I have gained honor for Myself over Pharaoh, his chariots, and his horsemen."

And the Angel of God, who went before the camp of Israel, moved and went behind them; and the pillar of cloud went from before them and stood behind them. So it came between the camp of the Egyptians and the camp of Israel. Thus it was a cloud and darkness TO THE ONE, and it gave light by night TO THE OTHER, so that the one did not come near the other all that night.

Then Moses stretched out his hand over the sea; and the LORD caused the sea to go BACK by a strong east wind all that night, and made the sea into dry

LAND, and the waters were divided. So the children of Israel went into the midst of the sea on the dry GROUND, and the waters WERE a wall to them on their right hand and on their left. And the Egyptians pursued and went after them into the midst of the sea, all Pharaoh's horses, his chariots, and his horsemen.

 Now it came to pass, in the morning watch, that the LORD looked down upon the army of the Egyptians through the pillar of fire and cloud, and He troubled the army of the Egyptians. And He took off their chariot wheels, so that they drove them with difficulty; and the Egyptians said, "Let us flee from the face of Israel, for the LORD fights for them against the Egyptians."

Then the LORD said to Moses, "Stretch out your hand over the sea, that the waters may come back upon the Egyptians, on their chariots, and on their horsemen." And Moses stretched out his hand over the sea; and when the morning appeared, the sea returned to its full depth, while the Egyptians were fleeing into it. So the LORD overthrew the Egyptians in the midst of the sea. Then the waters returned and covered the chariots, the horsemen, AND all the army of Pharaoh that came into the sea after them. Not so much as one of them remained. But the children of Israel had walked on dry LAND in the midst of the sea, and the waters WERE a wall to them on their right hand and on their left.

So the LORD saved Israel that day out of the hand of the Egyptians, and Israel saw the Egyptians dead on the seashore. Thus Israel saw the great work which the LORD had done in Egypt; so the people feared the LORD, and believed the LORD and His servant Moses.

EXODUS 15:1-23 Then Moses and the children of Israel sang this song to the LORD, and spoke, saying: "I will sing to the LORD, For He has triumphed gloriously! The horse and its rider He has thrown into the sea! The LORD IS my strength and song, And He has become my salvation; He IS my God, and I will praise Him; My father's God, and I will exalt Him.The LORD IS a man of war; The LORD IS His name. Pharaoh's chariots and his army He has cast into the sea; His chosen captains also are drowned in the Red Sea. The depths have covered them; They sank to the bottom like a stone."Your right hand, O LORD, has become glorious in power;

You have overthrown those who rose against You;

You sent forth Your wrath; It consumed them like stubble. And with the blast of Your nostrils The waters were gathered together; The floods stood upright like a heap; The depths congealed in the heart of the sea. The enemy said, 'I will pursue, I will overtake, I will divide the spoil; My desire shall be satisfied on them. I will draw my sword, My hand shall destroy them.' You blew with Your wind, The sea covered them; They sank like lead in the mighty waters.

"Who IS like You, O LORD, among the gods? Who IS like You, glorious in holiness, Fearful in praises, doing wonders? You stretched out Your right hand; The earth swallowed them. You in Your mercy have led forth The people whom You have redeemed; You have guided THEM in Your strength To Your holy habitation.

"The people will hear AND be afraid; Sorrow will take hold of the inhabitants of Philistia. Then the chiefs of Edom will be dismayed; The mighty men of Moab, Trembling will take hold of them; All the inhabitants of Canaan will melt away. Fear and dread will fall on them; By the greatness of Your arm They will be AS still as a stone, Till Your people pass over, O LORD, Till the people pass over Whom You have purchased. You will bring them in and plant them In the mountain of Your inheritance, IN the place, O LORD, WHICH You have made For Your own dwelling, The sanctuary, O Lord, WHICH Your hands have established.

"The LORD shall reign forever and ever."

For the horses of Pharaoh went with his chariots and his horsemen into the sea, and the LORD brought back the waters of the sea upon them. But the children of Israel went on dry LAND in the midst of the sea.

<u>The Song of Miriam</u>

Then Miriam the prophetess, the sister of Aaron, took the timbrel in her hand; and all the women went out after her with timbrels and with dances. And Miriam answered them:

"Sing to the LORD,

For He has triumphed gloriously!

The horse and its rider

He has thrown into the sea!"

Psalm 105:16-21 Moreover He called for a famine in the land; He destroyed all the provision of bread. He sent a man before them—Joseph—*who* was sold as a slave. They hurt his feet with fetters, He was laid in irons. Until the time that his word came to pass, The word of the LORD tested him. The king sent and released him, The ruler of the people let him go free. He made him lord of his house,

Genesis 40:9-15 Then the chief butler told his dream to Joseph, and said to him, "Behold, in my dream a vine *was* before me, and in the vine *were* three branches; it *was* as though it budded, its blossoms shot forth, and its clusters brought forth ripe grapes. Then Pharaoh's cup *was* in my hand; and I took the grapes and pressed them into Pharaoh's cup, and placed the cup in Pharaoh's hand." And Joseph said to him, "This *is* the interpretation of it: The three branches *are* three days. Now within three days Pharaoh will lift up your head and restore you to your place, and you will put Pharaoh's cup in his hand according to the former manner, when you were his butler. But remember me when it is well with you, and please show kindness to me; make mention of me to Pharaoh, and get me out of this house. For indeed I was stolen away from the land of the Hebrews; and also I have done nothing here that they should put me into the dungeon."

Genesis 40:23 Yet the chief butler did not remember Joseph, but forgot him.

Genesis 41: 1 Then it came to pass, at the end of two full years, that Pharaoh had a dream; and behold, he stood by the river.

Genesis 45:4-8 Joseph said to his brothers, "Please come near to me." So they came near. Then he said: "I *am* Joseph your brother, whom you sold into Egypt. But now, do not therefore be grieved or angry with yourselves because you sold me here; for God sent me before you to preserve life. For these two years the famine *has been* in the land, and *there are* still five years in which *there will be* neither plowing nor harvesting. And God sent me before you to preserve a posterity for you in the earth, and to save your lives by a great deliverance. So now *it was* not you *who* sent me here, but God; and He has made me a father to Pharaoh, and lord of all his house, and a ruler throughout all the land of Egypt.

CHAPTER FOUR

STEP 4

MARAH – BITTER WATER

Scripture Text: Exodus 15:22-26

Surely it is not meant to be funny, but one verse after the singing and celebration of getting through the Red Sea and free from the Pharaoh and his army another big **"whY"** came up on the journey (Ex. 15:22). Moses brought the children out into the wilderness three days and they found no water. Then they came to a place called Marah. There was water there but they could not drink it because it was bitter. Immediately the people murmured against Moses.

Now a skeptic could read this and question whether God is cruel or has a sadistic sense of humor. But of everything we know of God that would not add up. God knows what He is doing. Once again it was not a deliberate attempt to hurt the people. It was God's way to bring to the surface those debilitating hurts in the people so that God could heal them and set them free.

This event took place three days after the great Red Sea crossing and deliverance. God planned another opportunity to minister deliverance to additional hurts they were carrying out of Egypt. He purposely planned that water not be available. Back in Ex. 6:6-8 God had promised to rid them of their bondage. **The second thing binding the children of Israel was bitterness.** This also goes with slavery. Every slave asks the question **whY** me? What makes you better than me? Every slave resents being a slave until something is dealt with in his own heart. Evidently God wanted to also deal with bitterness quickly. Bitterness is like a tree with deep roots. Once bitterness roots in our heart we are faced with a life of misery. Bitterness will flavor everything we produce. Perhaps nothing hurts us more personally, than bitterness. Bitterness of soul poisons every life experience. It causes us to be judgmental of everyone and accusatory of others in everyday life. When a bitter person gets hundred dollars, they'll wonder why they didn't get a thousand dollars. When something good happens they'll be resentful and attempt to sabotage their good fortune. When something bad happens they often say, "I told you so." A bitter person is often sick with various physical ailments. The Bible says bitterness can bring rottenness to our bones.

God purposely kept them from water, the most basic human need. We can go weeks without food, but only a few days without water. The question is **whY** would the Lord withhold water? As we watch what God did next we will see that the discomfort was intended to be temporary. The people murmured and Moses cried out to God. God showed Moses a tree, which when cast into the water sweetened the water making it potable. The scripture then says that God was testing the people! This is uncomfortable. If He tests us that means we are accountable. Silver or gold is tested by putting it in the fire to find what is precious and what is common. Only the impure comes to the surface to be burned away, and what remains is pure.

By withholding water God had their undivided attention. He had made a provision to minister to their bitterness. He declared, "If you will diligently obey my voice and do that which is right in my sight, and listen to what I tell you to do, then I will not put any diseases on you that are on the Egyptians." Lastly he declared, "I am the Lord who heals you."

We would all rather have life's lessons taught in a classroom setting where we can agree or disagree with the teacher. But God uses life's circumstances as our classroom. There was no debate. They were parched, panting for water. They were in a place to agree with God to do whatever it took to satisfy their thirst.

They were a bitter people, and understandably so. He is a healing God. In order to get to the Promised Land, they needed bitterness healed. The bigger the test is then the more important the lesson. You can sit in the classroom to learn the rules of driving a car. But the true test comes behind the wheel and on the road. A pilot can study the charts and know math calculations, but the proof is in flying the plane. Withholding water from over two million people to minister a truth would have to be an important life changing principle. Unfortunately, we can miss invaluable lessons from God by not seeing them as a test for our benefit.

The children of Israel used these places of desperation as a time of complaining about God and Moses. They demanded that their needs be met.

They were judging God because they assumed He failed them because they came to this place with no water. They expected to have water and food whenever they were thirsty or hungry. From God's perspective it was the other way around. He brought them to places of physical need to make them aware of their spiritual and emotional needs. By creating physical needs, he brought them to a place of healing. He eventually provided for their physical needs as well.

So let's get this straight. *For the second time God purposely led the children of Israel to a place of human need that was beyond human solution.* The need was something in the natural realm, which had supernatural implications. God was using physical needs and complications to reveal their need for healing. By using a tree to sweeten the water, He was revealing *The Tree of Life*, which was only available in Him. His life in them would sweeten their lives, regardless of past experiences.

God never apologized for Marah. He did not make a mistake. Moses had not failed. And surely it was not to hurt the people. To the contrary, it was a well-laid plan -- for healing and equipping for future service. It was the key revelation to the character of God. They were being trained to serve Him so they could rule and reign in the Promised Land. He said, "I am the God that heals thee." In a world of sickness and disease -- what a great revelation! We worship a God that heals!

Our places of panic over unfulfilled needs can be for good or bad. The benefits seem to be dependent on our attitude of how we respond to God. Again we are talking about perspective. From their point of view, three days without water for over two million people was a crisis. It was critical from an individual point of view, as well as from the corporate point of view. If faced with this dilemma how would we respond? Murmuring and complaining reveals a lack of trust in God. It reveals a hardness of heart that births unbelief. But let's be careful. Thirty five hundred years later, it seems easy to calculate how they should have responded to God and the circumstances He was leading them through.

But the fact remains that each one of us comes to places of crisis on our life's journey. We must not be limited by our narrow personal perspective, but consider God's point of view. Personally, I could see myself standing in that wilderness and admitting to being very thirsty. At that moment I have a choice; to blame someone or to trust that something else must be at work, regardless of how it feels, knowing it will be for good. What would have happened if the people came to that moment of great need and began a praise service just like the one on the "other side" of the Red Sea? What if they would have believed that God was in total control -- that He was going to do something supernatural for their good? What if they would have merely trusted Him?

Let us acknowledge that their pain was great. They were a bitter people. But they probably did not realize how deep those roots were buried. After three days of dryness they come to water too bitter to drink. By living life on a higher plane, we could see that there is more to life than meets the eye. We would see that bitter water was a message to heal and not to hurt. But it felt like hurt. On the spiritual level it was to heal, now and forever. God was not after the symptoms of bitterness, He was digging out the bitter root. This required major surgery in psyche of the people. A pill will pacify the symptom. Surgery is an example of the ultimate cutting away. There is no growing the problem back after it has been painfully extracted. In our western church, there is a preoccupation with the victim; too much time is spent pacifying life's hurts. God wants to cut them out. We tend to spare someone of suffering, but God uses the pains of life to root out the problems that hurt us.

While God proved He would heal, He is about to do something never before witnessed in human history. He declared that He would keep the camp free from all sickness and disease for the entire journey! Just imagine the miracle of millions of people traveling for forty years without sickness and disease, (although later, many died as a result of deliberate acts of disobedience or unbelief.) During this journey, their shoes and clothes did not wear out either. The people were initially looking at this three days without water as harsh and cruel. But God was looking at it as a means to reveal Himself to His people in a way never known to Mankind. He was consistently proving Himself as their provider who was healing and caring for His people. They were walking in health as no other people anywhere else in history.

As God revealed the benefits of a relationship with Him, He also used this time to lay down some fresh requirements for His people. God is on stage at one of the most dramatic moments in history. He has the full attention of over two million people who were on the verge of dying of thirst. Along with the healing promise, He lays down specific expectations on His people (Ex. 15:26). He says, "I want you to carefully and attentively listen to what I have to say, and I want you to do what I tell you. In addition, I want you to do what is right in MY SIGHT." God had a powerful message early on in this journey. Remember that they are only a few days out of Egypt. And while He is healing them, He is also trying to change their orientation to life. Instead of trying to get Him to anticipate their needs and making them go away - He wants them to *trust Him for everything* -- to see things from His point of view.

This is a powerful and life changing challenge. This is a worldview correction that God is trying to instill in His people. He does not want them looking at their world from the viewpoint of a slave. He wants them see the world with the understanding that He is King of kings and Lord of lords and that they are His people and He is their God.

It was the next step in the unfolding of His goodness, love and care for His people. So far in this journey, Almighty God has communicated to His people that He would show them more of Himself. His name was newly revealed as the "I AM." The "I AM" declares that God is the same yesterday, today, and forever. The "I AM" authorized them to get out of Egypt. At the Red Sea, He showed them His Salvation. God proved Himself more powerful than their enemies. His authority supersedes natural phenomena like wind, storms, and seas. Now, here at Marah, He was revealing Himself as the Lord that Heals. The Lord that Heals also has expectations on His people. As God was using this pilgrimage as a time to show the people more of Him so they could better identify with Him, at the same time He was defining further expectations He was placing on His people.

God was expecting His people to begin to look at life from His point of view. Today, we would call this a paradigm shift. God was saying that your old belief system will not get you into the Promised Land. You have learned to rely on yourselves to get through daily life. Your success has been determined by whether you feel good about things. As a slave you have been content with enough food and water and tolerable working conditions. Now these are no longer the yardsticks for success. God was saying that how you feel is no longer the criteria for success.

The shift He was looking for the people to make was to find out - how does God look at this situation? What does God see here? What does God want to happen in this time? What is God trying to get at?

Back to the shores of Marah, their question was **whY** is there no water? God was using life's circumstances, planned and arranged by Him, to reveal the deep issues of the heart. Through this revelation they could learn to rely on Him and His character. For every need, He has a solution. For every hurt, He has a healing. It took pressure to bring the needs out into the open. That's why this **whY** was in their journey. We can be wondering **whY** He did not have the water in the ready. What deeper significance is at work here?

Notice that again He did not take them back to analyze why they were bitter. He did not spend a single sentence in the scripture determining why they were bitter, or explaining why they had reason to be. He was going to do something about it. Once again, through a crisis, emotions were forced to the surface. Belief systems detrimental to their future were exposed. Fear and bitterness will keep us from finding God's life promises for us. As a people, He wanted to set them free so that they could go on. God could not have used Joseph as long as bitterness was held in his heart. Likewise, these people could not possess the Promised Land while they were in bondage to fear and bitterness. God orchestrated this journey down to the minutest detail in order to show them the way to freedom. God needed to change their belief system, so that they could be free from the slave mentality to walk in the ruling and reigning mentality of the Kingdom of God here on earth.

May God reveal and set each of us free from fear and bitterness – key enemies to our soul?

SCRIPTURES FOR THIS CHAPTER

EXODUS 15:22-26 So Moses brought Israel from the Red Sea; then they went out into the Wilderness of Shur. And they went three days in the wilderness and found no water. Now when they came to Marah, they could not drink the waters of Marah, for they WERE bitter. Therefore the name of it was called Marah. And the people complained against Moses, saying, "What shall we drink?" So he cried out to the LORD, and the LORD showed him a tree. When he cast IT into the waters, the waters were made sweet.

There He made a statute and an ordinance for them, and there He tested them, and said, "If you diligently heed the voice of the LORD your God and do what is right in His sight, give ear to His commandments and keep all His statutes, I will put none of the diseases on you which I have brought on the Egyptians. For I AM the LORD who heals you."

EXODUS 6:6-8 Therefore say to the children of Israel: 'I *am* the LORD; I will bring you out from under the burdens of the Egyptians, I will rescue you from their bondage, and I will redeem you with an outstretched arm and with great judgments. I will take you as My people, and I will be your God. Then you shall know that I *am* the LORD your God who brings you out from under the burdens of the Egyptians. And I will bring you into the land which I swore to give to Abraham, Isaac, and Jacob; and I will give it to you *as* a heritage: I *am* the LORD.'"

CHAPTER FIVE

STEP 5

ELIM – R & R

Scripture Text: Exodus 15:27

The more we learn of God, the more we discover that His mercies are new every morning. Great is His faithfulness. Great is His compassion. He is trying to move the children of Israel physically, emotionally, and psychologically from their slavery experience to rulers in a land flowing with milk and honey. He is using the journey to convert their way of thinking to learn to think His way. Each place of difficulty is an opportunity to learn and flourish under His care and authority. It is essential for their success. The last verse of Exodus 15 says He immediately took them to Elim from Marah. Elim had twelve wells of water – one for each tribal group. Also, there were seventy palm trees, a virtual oasis in the desert to accommodate over two million souls. He was providing a time of refreshing to comfort His people on their way to the place of Promise.

They had just endured two major confrontations with life changing consequences. God chose to then give them a respite. But the question coming was how they would use this time that was intended to help them regroup and get ready for the balance of the journey.

We will see the children of Israel had a complaint on their lips as soon as the journey began again. In fact, the complaint was so focused on human leadership, we know what they did in Elim – they measured the man leading them, rather than rehearse the wonderful provision and character of God. They looked back at their few days of journey and complained about how bad it was rather than how good the results were. Instead of recognizing all that God had done for them, they murmured about why did He not have all things prepared for them when they got to the places of need? They thought the path through the Red Sea should have been waiting for them. They thought the water should already have been sweet when they got there.

How do we relate to the Lord and connect with Him when the going is tough? A better question can be how do we relate to God in a time of refreshing and rest? From the context of scripture, the Lord was bringing the people to a revelation of the Sabbath. Right after a wrenching exposure to bitterness, He was giving them some "time off" from pressures of change and decision-making under duress. The oasis of Elim was such a time to gather themselves and comfort one another. It was a time to rest in God and consider all that He had done with them. He let them be refreshed for forty two days. It was intended as a time to be strengthened and be built up for the rest of the journey.

Unfortunately, the response to the next step after Elim reveals that they sat around and complained during what was supposed to be their time of rest. As we look at the history of people relating to God, we see that in the hard times they turned and relied upon Him. But, in the good times, the historical record will bear out that people at best, drift away from Him. Sometimes, they have quickly turned to false gods or to deeper sin.

But the question to every generation is what about us and how do we handle the time off from crisis? As a nation, we had been at "Elim" starting in the 1970's and throughout the 1990's. How did we use the time of refreshment and rest? It would not be fair to indict the whole Church, but the evidence of positive results was bleak. Although much had been done overseas in the Church, the results on the home front were weak. In the last twenty years, more people have been saved than in the last thousand years worldwide. There are reports of tremendous revival from China to South America to Africa. The former Soviet Union had come to revival during the 1990's with the Church making great inroads in the youth of that nation.

But in America, it seems we used the time of rest as a time to go the way of the world. In the seventies, eighties, and nineties we spent so much time and money condemning our culture. But after the turn of the century, we see the culture is in worse condition than before. The Church mirrors our culture in too many negative respects. Pre-marital sex, divorce, alcohol, drugs, living together, financial irregularities, pornography etc. is in some cases just as rampant in the Church as in the culture. Rather than the Church impacting the culture, evidence reveals that the impact has been the other way around. In a time of blessing it is easy to neglect and lose sight of God. Many would argue that God had nothing to do with this time of prosperity. However, history shows that we are only a "good rumor" away from financial collapse. Clearly, in this first decade, our level of prosperity has shown how fragile we are, more fragile than we would be willing to admit. The amazing point is there is nothing we can do about it on our own either.

The events of September 11, 2001 have proven how unstable our world leading security is in America. The catastrophic assaults on our nation could have driven us closer to God. Many consider it was a time to declare a wakeup call to America -- for the church to repent of spiritual lethargy. But there is no evidence that has happened – yet.

But what should the Church do in a time of rest? We have cried wolf so long, our culture won't listen to any more condemnation or criticism from the Church. The children of Israel used the time to gossip and complain. The evidence points out that we are doing the same in this day and age. When Jesus came to the woman at the well (John 4) He asked her for a drink. As they continued talking, Jesus said, "If you knew who I really was you would ask me for a drink." The woman went to the natural way of "looking at things," by challenging His ability to get her a drink. She challenged Him because He had no utensil to draw water. He responded by saying, "If you drink the water I have to give, you will never thirst again because the water I have to give shall be a well of water that will spring up into everlasting life."

Water carries a significant spiritual connotation in life. The woman at the well was engaging Christ on the natural level she could "see." Christ was engaging her in conversation from God's point of view. Water and life go hand in hand. Jesus explained that there is a "new kind of water" coming. She immediately took the conversation to a spiritual level by asking about the experience of worship. The first response, of all people in scripture, when they were in the Presence of the Lord, was to respond in worship.

What should the children of Israel have done while they were at Elim? What should the Church be doing whenever she experiences her time of Elim? We better free up the spiritual well that is within us. Let us take our eyes off of the shortcomings of the Church and the world. Our focus needs to be on our worship with the Lord. Isaac came to a place where his father had dug sixteen wells. Others had used these wells after the departure of Abraham, and then the Philistines stopped them up. But Isaac came and re-dug the wells, so that the water would flow freely and bring the prosperity to the herds. The Lord was able to prosper him and all that was his (Gen.26: 15). It is time for the

Church to "dig up the wells" and renew our worship in heart and mind of the Lord.

Jesus tells us that if "any thirst let them come to Him and drink." Because, "out of his belly shall flow rivers of living water" (John 7:37-39). What is Jesus essentially talking about? He is talking about the Holy Spirit. It seems the American Church has been trying to use the Holy Spirit to do things *for them*; however, the proper function of the Holy Spirit is that He wants to do things *in them*. Instead of sitting around to gossip and criticize, let us use this time in the Church to unstop our wells of living waters through the Holy Spirit. It is a time for us to yield to Him, serve Him, love Him and worship Him. Let's be grateful for what He has done for us.

While the children of Israel were at Elim, it was an opportunity to walk in the revelation of the Lord and what He had just imparted to them. It was a time to seal the work of God in their lives. The way to do that is the assembling ourselves together for corporate worship. By coming together, we can encourage one another and challenge one another to live for God. Rest is a time of discipline. Not time to kick back and take it easy. It is the time to be diligent and learn the disciplines of the faith. It is a time to be careful and restrain activity and worship God. Without the pressure and demands of immediate needs, it is time to prepare for future needs. It is a time to know God and establish the ability to walk in the Spirit.

An army uses the time of rest in battle to refill the supply lines, to gather resources, to heal the sick, and to repair the broken places. We surely know that the battle is not over. God has yet to have the glory of the Lord fill the Earth. He will do that through the Church. In order to manifest His glory, the Church must set their heart on Him. The Church must give the Holy Spirit free reign anew. It must unstop all those activities that the enemy has used to stop the wells of life in the Church.

This time of blessing in America is an opportunity to be established in the faith. It is time for prayer, fasting and diligence in the Word of God.

A time of blessing is a time to be on guard. Give the enemy no quarter. Don't give the devil an inch. Guard your mouth and heart. Diligently study His word. Get to know the Lord in ways that you don't know Him. Discover who He is in your life. The increased knowledge of Him will change your life. Other than a handful of exceptions, the American church is hard pressed to get a one percent extended participation in a prayer meeting. Disciplined ongoing classes that require homework, memory work, and faithful attendance get small turnouts. There was a time that a Bible course required nine months to complete with no excuse for missing a class, and people would flock to sign up. Now, most Bible teachers have to keep finding ways to entice people to even sign up, let alone attend such a class. Nine months – forget it, people are looking for two weeks. The standards are falling by the wayside. May the Lord revive our hearts today for the truth of Jesus Christ?

Unfortunately, there is more grumbling going on in church than in the world. In one denomination, one thousand pastors per month are dropping out of the ministry. Pastors are spending more time dealing with the politics of the Church rather than the Word of the Lord. We, as a people, must come back to the Lord in a very unusual way.

At Elim, we must make a renewed commitment to the Lord. We must do all we can to resist the temptation of criticizing others. We must build leaders, pastors and not tear them down. We must set aside a time to fast, read our Word, memorize scripture, pray and serve others. Replenish the supply lines. Let us find the next leaders and begin to raise them up to serve the Lord. It is the day to give ourselves to the youth of the church (and to the youth of the culture). It is a time to raise up the next generation of leaders. It is the day to mentor and father young men in the ways of the Lord.

In a time of peace, the military gets out all the old disciplines of polishing shoes, dressing, saluting, marching in cadence, memory work, and learning how to wage battle. They learn how to follow authority, even if they don't agree with authority. Why does the military do these things in a time of peace? So that in the time of war, they will know the principles of how to follow, and what it takes in order to win. In actual battle you don't worry about shining your shoes, or whether your uniform is pressed. You don't march in cadence, nor do you salute your officers. These are training disciplines that prepare us for the hardships of battle.

Perhaps the Church is being too slack. But, in the military you are dealing with an army that is on the payroll. There are stripes to be earned in peacetime, so there is a motivation to follow the disciplines of the army. The Church is an all-volunteer army. Yes, there are paid staffs, but when it comes right down to it; the volunteers normally give them very little authority. The volunteers normally do not have a mindset of an army in training.

Yet, to go with God to the place He is leading, to walk in all of His promises for this life, we must develop a different mindset. We are in a war that is actually a life and death struggle. We must practice the disciplines of the faith. Men like Daniel have set the pattern. He was a man on the rise in the government of a nation. Yet, he took three times per day, probably one hour each time, to seek his Lord in prayer. King David even got up at midnight to pray. The Church has all the teaching manuals it needs. We have all the Bible versions we need. We have all the classes we need, and all the opportunities that are necessary to know God. What we need are more people willing to place themselves under authority and make renewed commitments to the disciplines of the faith.

There is recognition in the Church to open up expressions of worship in many denominations that resisted change in this area. But let us not substitute methods for genuine heartfelt revelation and experience in worshipping the Lord. Jesus said that we are to worship the Father and Him only are we to *serve*. We need the revelation of *service worship* to be renewed in the Church and in our hearts. It is time to use our time and energy to serve the Lord. It is time to walk in the daily disciplines of the faith. We need more dedicated people who will set their heart and give their time to building up and strengthening the Church.

Will you be one of those?

SCRIPTURES USED FOR THIS CHAPTER

EXODUS 15:27 Then they came to Elim, where there *were* twelve wells of water and seventy palm trees; so they camped there by the waters.

John 4:7-15 A woman of Samaria came to draw water. Jesus said to her, "Give Me a drink." For His disciples had gone away into the city to buy food. Then the woman of Samaria said to Him, "How is it that You, being a Jew, ask a drink from me, a Samaritan woman?" For Jews have no dealings with Samaritans.

Jesus answered and said to her, "If you knew the gift of God, and who it is who says to you, 'Give Me a drink,' you would have asked Him, and He would have given you living water." The woman said to Him, "Sir, You have nothing to draw with, and the well is deep. Where then do You get that living water? Are You greater than our father Jacob, who gave us the well, and drank from it himself, as well as his sons and his livestock?"

Jesus answered and said to her, "Whoever drinks of this water will thirst again, but whoever drinks of the water that I shall give him will never thirst. But the water that I shall give him will become in him a fountain of water springing up into everlasting life." The woman said to Him, "Sir, give me this water, that I may not thirst, nor come here to draw."

John 4:19-26 The woman said to Him, "Sir, I perceive that You are a prophet. Our fathers worshiped on this mountain, and you *Jews* say that in Jerusalem is the place where one ought to worship."

Jesus said to her, "Woman, believe Me, the hour is coming when you will neither on this mountain, nor in Jerusalem, worship the Father. You worship what you do not know; we know what we worship, for salvation is of the Jews. But the hour is coming, and now is, when the true worshipers will worship the Father in spirit and truth; for the Father is seeking such to worship Him. God *is* Spirit, and those who worship Him must worship in spirit and truth." The woman said to Him, "I know that Messiah is coming" (who is called Christ). "When He comes, He will tell us all things." Jesus said to her, "I who speak to you am *He.*

John 7:37-39 On the last day, that great *day* of the feast, Jesus stood and cried out, saying, "If anyone thirsts, let him come to Me and drink. He who believes in Me, as the Scripture has said, out of his heart will flow rivers of living water." But this He spoke concerning the Spirit, whom those believing n Him would receive; for the Holy Spirit was not yet *given,* because Jesus was not yet glorified.

CHAPTER SIX

STEP 6

WILDERNESS OF SIN

Scripture Text: Exodus 16:1-17:6

Exodus 16 is the setting for the next key step of training on the journey to the Promised Land. The Lord gave them a rest at Elim for forty-two days. A respite if you will. It could have been a perfect time to regroup and to allow the changes to take root. A time for relationships to be better understood. A time to come to grips with the Lord who was leading them. Moments in rest, to better understand how trustworthy He is. Forty-two is a number of some Biblical significance. Used in other places to define the number of weeks of years before Messiah. It is also the number of months for the tribulation. In any event, it was enough time for them to gather themselves after the traumatic time at Marah and go forward.

Unfortunately, they used these forty two days to sit around and complain. Oddly, their complaints focused on the men who God had called to lead them out of Egypt and into the Promised Land. As we read verse two, it seems that out of nowhere, they murmur against Moses and Aaron. We can almost hear Moses and Aaron respond to each other, "What did we do?"

The people were frustrated. We don't know what they ate for the forty five days since they left Egypt, but they ate something. They had not complained about food before this, except when they wanted meat. However, there was now a definite lack. This stirred in them another major problem. Rising out of their hearts was a new bitter complaint. It came as an accusation against leadership. This stirred up the fear that they were going to die in the wilderness. Again they rehearsed how good it was for them in Egypt! Our minds can surely play tricks on us.

The Lord came to Moses with news that He would rain bread from heaven on them six days per week for the remainder of the journey. God put **two stipulations** on what the people called "manna." One requirement was that each family could only gather enough for their family for the day – no hoarding. Secondly, each family on the sixth day was to gather a two-day supply, to provide for the Sabbath Day. God was making the Sabbath Day a formal day of rest and devotion to God by the people.

So, the Lord once again let a physical need be the means to reveal what was in the hearts of the people. Once again God was showing them through their physical need that they also had a deep inner need. This time that inner need revolved around their misunderstanding of relating to human authority. We could try to make an excuse for them, and ask how could a slave group of people understand how to relate to authority in a healthy way? The problem with that reasoning is the Lord did not offer that excuse for the people. From God's point of view, the pressure He brought about food and the lack thereof was for the purpose to show Himself in a new and exciting way to the people. But, they could not see past their belly to even look for the goodness of God.

The Lord did again what He had done before: He released His provision to meet the physical needs and also provided to minister to their spiritual needs. As we look back we have to come to grips with the truth that God, in His infinite wisdom once again withheld from the people a fundamental human need – food – first water and now food. Here we are at another big **whY** in the road.

After the rules of gathering manna are put in place we can begin to see the lessons involved. The first thing Moses talks about is that this provision will prove that it was the Lord who brought you out of Egypt. Evidently the people began to focus on Earthly leadership and before you know it the people had talked themselves into thinking that this journey was Moses and Aaron's idea! So Moses found it necessary to use the evidence of manna as proof that it is the Lord that is leading them. Moses continues the argument and says that in the morning when you see continued provision you will see the glory of the Lord. Then Moses gets into this argument "what are we that you murmur against us." Moses was saying in today's vernacular "get a life," he went on "your argument is not with us it is with God. You may be complaining about us but I have news for you, you are really complaining about God."

Then Moses, through Aaron, gathered the people before the Lord, because he warned them that the Lord heard their murmuring. They gathered and looked toward the wilderness, and God put on what must have been a glorious display of Himself. It says that they looked and the glory of the Lord appeared to them. Now over the last forty years I have heard many say if we could just see the Lord, if He would just show us something of Himself we would love it and it would do wonders for our faith. However, in this passage we are given no reaction from the people for this display. I take that to mean that no appreciable response was forthcoming. The scripture is careful to say that the "whole" congregation saw the manifestation of the Lord. The next thing to happen here was the Lord spoke to Moses and said He heard the murmuring of the people. He then said flesh would be on the menu tonight – quail would be flown in, and the next morning bread would be supplied. He makes a profound statement next. He says "then shall you know that I am the Lord your God."

Evidently there was an identity crisis in the camp. When we don't know who we are it is because we don't know who God is. There has always been a philosophy around that we need to go out and find ourselves. But that is not true. The evidence is that God engineered this whY in the road to bring to them the realization that He is not only God, but also that He is **their** God. There is a big difference between the two. We can say Jesus is **THE** Savior but the real question is can we say Jesus is **MY** Savior. The devil knows Jesus is **THE** Savior, but he is going to hell. The Lord was using this journey again to help them come to grips with who He is, and then they would know who they were.

When we "know" the qualities and character of God then it doesn't matter who we are. We can take comfort in the fact that if we come up short in anything that, as we know God, we will know that He will make up for whatever we lack. If we are not strong enough, as we know Him we will find out the He is made strong in our weakness. If we are poor we can find that He is the Lord that provides. If we don't know what to say, He will give us the Holy Spirit to give us the words. In the human way of looking at things, we want Him to hide our weaknesses. But God wants to show those weaknesses so that He will be glorified in our lives. God in His goodness withheld food so that the people could be convinced, in their own personal experience that He is **their** Lord.

Well, God established the rules regarding the distribution pattern for the food. Wouldn't we know it; some of the children immediately broke the rules and gathered more manna than they needed for one day? Evidently it took a little effort and some said "if we have gone to all the trouble to be out here why not save tomorrow's trip and gather more and save ourselves the effort." But that which they hoarded turned to worms and stank, literally, to high heaven, evidently smelling up the camp. But the double gathering on the sixth day was according to the rules and the point was made that the Lord miraculously preserved the manna an additional day because that additional day was to take precedence over the rule of one-day supply.

So, the Lord was affirming that He is their God and also making provision for the present and future journey for food. If we consider the amount of food required for over two million people daily we can see the plan is an incredible and miraculous plan. I don't know what you imagine the wilderness to look like, but having been in the specific area I can tell you it looks like the moon. There is not a tree in sight that is why the seventy palm trees at Elim were a big deal. There are no streams, no bushes, and no wildlife. It is one of the most desolate places on the earth.

The Lord's plan shut off all earthly provisions for the journey. It was His intention that the people would learn to depend upon Him and none other. While He has created us with great capacities to survive, and to find a way to make do in many situations, He was shutting them off from all self-reliance by not making available any natural resources. It was His plan to teach them how to look to Him for provision. He wanted them to see how much He loved them and cared for them. He wanted them to see that He would lead and provide for them. He wanted them to see that when they had a question that He was the answer.

In addition, He was establishing one day per week that was for the purpose of developing their relationship with Him. Even as He established the Sabbath as a day of rest and devotion, initially some of the children went out to gather manna on this Sabbath. God said to Moses "How long will you refuse to keep my commandments and laws?" God reiterated that the Sabbath was a gift. It may be true that slaves have trouble receiving gifts but now the Lord expected them to so receive. He also expected them to stay in their place or tent and this to be a family day for the purpose of jointly spending time with the Lord.

As we know later, the Lord included in the Ten Commandments, that they were to remember the Sabbath and keep it Holy. He was telling the children that their relationship with Him required time together. In fact, the relationship was so vital that He was declaring that He expected them to set aside one seventh of their life for Him! The relationship is complicated and takes time and effort on our part to interact with Him to discover more about Him. His ways are not our ways and His thoughts are not our thoughts., We must with time and effort, learn His ways and thoughts.

The present day statistics say that almost half of the Christians in America don't open their Bible monthly to read His Word. The statistics are that probably only one quarter to one third of Christians regularly attends church. But, God said to the children of Israel that you need to spend one seventh of your life with Me. One day per week – not home watching sports either. This is fifty two days per year plus daily prayer and daily reading of His Word. We will see later that He also called them to spend twenty one more days per year at various times of feasting and celebration of His involvement in their lives. Now out of these twenty one days they include three Sabbath days. The net result was that the Lord expected seventy days of the year to be set aside for him! To consider this another way God was going to bring them to the place that they were to devote nearly twenty percent of their time with Him!

Oh Lord, help us this day to find our way of relationship with You? The revelation of manna was a lesson so significant to the Lord that He had Moses take and gather a pot of manna and keep it as a memorial to carry with them on the rest of the journey. He preserved this manna because He wanted the children to always be reminded of His provision. Manna is a key Biblical theme for all God's people down through the centuries. It shows us by example that He is the bread of life. It is in Him that we live and move and have our being. Manna is bread from heaven. It connects us to Him and it always means life. With Him we find life and life more abundantly. Jesus so magnified this principle that He declared that He is the bread of life. He later declared about the bread that it is His body and that we are to take and eat His body which was broken for us.

We see that manna was more than something to eat daily for the children of Israel; it was a principle of relationship between the Lord and His people. It speaks of the limitations of the earthly natural resources in the context of eternity. It shows all mankind that unless there is heavenly intervention that our resources will not last and the end is death. Manna is a picture that our Lord is the bread of life. His life is eternal.

Before we leave this sixth step let's come back to a very humanly conceived fallacy. People seem to always conclude that their need means that someone failed them. When they needed water they complained to Moses and accused him and God of not providing. Now the need for food stirred up rebellion in the camp. The focus of the gossip was leadership and leadership's failure to provide food. The motives of leadership came into question again with the expressed question, "Are we being led to slaughter in the wilderness?" As we can see from the Biblical account that Moses and Aaron had virtually nothing to say about these matters. They were not making any decisions about the journey's progress. They were unable to plan for food and water for there were no human provisions available or possible. They were responding to the moving of the cloud by day and the fire by night. Human leadership usually tries to respond to the leading of the Lord. That is what is supposed to happen.

For Moses and Aaron it was quite obvious that they were not ahead of the cloud or fire, proving they had no control over the needs of the people. This means that in order for the human leadership to anticipate the needs of the people and somehow find provision for them they would have had to disobey God. Often we think our leadership must have missed God because we have needs. The reality might be that if we don't have needs maybe leadership is missing God. God is in our needs. We just need to find Him.

Needs are not evidence that anyone missed God. Needs reveal what is in our heart. The question is not how I can avoid needs; the question is how I am going to react to my needs when they are made apparent. Often it takes a physical need to reveal that we have a spiritual need, that we have either been ignoring, or not been aware that we had such a need. Humanly, we often think the test of life is that I can live on a level that I don't have any needs. But the test of life is how I respond to my times of need.

Do I moan and groan and try to blame others? Do I blame those in authority over me; do I blame God, challenging Him that He should not have let me come to this place of need? Everyone on earth experiences times of great need. For eighty percent of the world their need revolves around food and water! The lessons in the wilderness have direct application. The other twenty percent have needs that are magnified in relationships, in temptations, in pressures revolving around their ability to gather finances and so on. Is it not true that whether you make Three thousand dollars per year, Thirty thousand dollars per year, or Three hundred thousand dollars per year that the only difference between the problems are some zeros at the end! God uses the pressures in life for us to find Him in new ways.

If we would take each confrontation with need as an opportunity to turn our heart to Him, we will find Him. If we would look at each time of need as a time to discover how He will bring a victory, we will find victory. He is there to help in time of need.

This step also settled the fact that when a need of the basics came forth that the Lord was behind it with a provision. In this case He settled that He would provide their food for the rest of the journey. There were rules in the gathering of the food that were required. Also don't forget that the Lord was giving them the Sabbath day for the development of their relationship with Him.

SCRIPTURES USED FOR THIS CHAPTER

EXODUS 16:1-36 And they journeyed from Elim, and all the congregation of the children of Israel came to the Wilderness of Sin, which is between Elim and Sinai, on the fifteenth day of the second month after they departed from the land of Egypt. Then the whole congregation of the children of Israel complained against Moses and Aaron in the wilderness. And the children of Israel said to them, "Oh, that we had died by the hand of the LORD in the land of Egypt, when we sat by the pots of meat AND when we ate bread to the full! For you have brought us out into this wilderness to kill this whole assembly with hunger."

Then the LORD said to Moses, "Behold, I will rain bread from heaven for you. And the people shall go out and gather a certain quota every day, that I may test them, whether they will walk in My law or not. And it shall be on the sixth day that they shall prepare what they bring in, and it shall be twice as much as they gather daily."

Then Moses and Aaron said to all the children of Israel, "At evening you shall know that the LORD has brought you out of the land of Egypt. And in the morning you shall see the glory of the LORD; for He hears your complaints against the LORD. But what ARE we, that you complain against us?" Also Moses said, "THIS SHALL BE SEEN when the LORD gives you meat to eat in the evening, and in the morning bread to the full; for the LORD hears your complaints which you make against Him. And what ARE we? Your complaints ARE not against us but against the LORD."

Then Moses spoke to Aaron, "Say to all the congregation of the children of Israel, 'Come near before the LORD, for He has heard your complaints.'" Now it came to pass, as Aaron spoke to the whole congregation of the children of Israel, that they looked toward the wilderness, and behold, the glory of the LORD appeared in the cloud.

And the LORD spoke to Moses, saying, "I have heard the complaints of the children of Israel. Speak to them, saying, 'At twilight you shall eat meat, and in the morning you shall be filled with bread. And you shall know that I AM the LORD your God.' "

So it was that quails came up at evening and covered the camp, and in the morning the dew lay all around the camp. And when the layer of dew lifted, there, on the surface of the wilderness, was a small round substance, AS fine as frost on the ground. So when the children of Israel saw IT, they said to one another, "What is it?" For they did not know what it WAS.

And Moses said to them, "This IS the bread which the LORD has given you to eat. This is the thing which the LORD has commanded: 'Let every man gather it according to each one's need, one omer for each person, ACCORDING TO THE number of persons; let every man take for THOSE who ARE in his tent.' "

Then the children of Israel did so and gathered, some more, some less. So when they measured IT by omers, he who gathered much had nothing left over, and he who gathered little had no lack. Every man had gathered according to each one's need. And Moses said, "Let no one leave any of it till morning." Notwithstanding they did not heed Moses. But some of them left part of it until morning, and it bred worms and stank. And Moses was angry with them. So they gathered it every morning, every man according to his need. And when the sun became hot, it melted.

And so it was, on the sixth day, THAT they gathered twice as much bread, two Omers for each one. And all the rulers of the congregation came and told Moses. Then he said to them, "This IS WHAT the LORD has said: 'Tomorrow IS a Sabbath rest, a holy Sabbath to the LORD. Bake what you will bake TODAY, and boil what you will boil; and lay up for yourselves all that remains, to be kept until morning.' " So they laid it up till morning, as Moses commanded; and it did not stink, nor were there any worms in it. Then Moses said, "Eat that today, for today IS a Sabbath to the LORD; today you will not find it in the field. Six days you shall gather it, but on the seventh day, the Sabbath, there will be none."

Now it happened THAT SOME of the people went out on the seventh day to gather, but they found none. And the LORD said to Moses, "How long do you refuse to keep My commandments and My laws? See! For the LORD has given you the Sabbath; therefore He gives you on the sixth day bread for two days. Let every man remain in his place; let no man go out of his place on the seventh day." So the people rested on the seventh day.

And the house of Israel called its name Manna. And it WAS like white coriander seed, and the taste of it WAS like wafers MADE with honey.

Then Moses said, "This IS the thing which the LORD has commanded: 'Fill an omer with it, to be kept for your generations, that they may see the bread with which I fed you in the wilderness, when I brought you out of the land of Egypt.'" And Moses said to Aaron, "Take a pot and put an omer of manna in it, and lay it up before the LORD, to be kept for your generations." As the LORD commanded Moses, so Aaron laid it up before the Testimony, to be kept. And the children of Israel ate manna forty years, until they came to an inhabited land; they ate manna until they came to the border of the land of Canaan. Now an omer IS one-tenth of an ephah.

EXODUS 17:1-7 Then all the congregation of the children of Israel set out on their journey from the Wilderness of Sin, according to the commandment of the LORD, and camped in Rephidim; but THERE WAS no water for the people to drink. Therefore the people contended with Moses, and said, "Give us water, that we may drink."

So Moses said to them, "Why do you contend with me? Why do you tempt the LORD?"

And the people thirsted there for water, and the people complained against Moses, and said, "Why IS it you have brought us up out of Egypt, to kill us and our children and our livestock with thirst?"

So Moses cried out to the LORD, saying, "What shall I do with this people? They are almost ready to stone me!"

And the LORD said to Moses, "Go on before the people, and take with you some of the elders of Israel. Also take in your hand your rod with which you struck the river, and go. Behold, I will stand before you there on the rock in Horeb; and you shall strike the rock, and water will come out of it that the people may drink."

And Moses did so in the sight of the elders of Israel. So he called the name of the place Massah and Meribah, because of the contention of the children of Israel, and because they tempted the LORD, saying, "Is the LORD among us or not?"

CHAPTER SEVEN

STEP 7

REPHIDEM— AGAIN?

Scripture Text: Exodus 17:1- 18: 27

Sometime between the forty fifth day out of Egypt and the ninetieth day out of Egypt the children were commanded by God to go to the wilderness called Rephidim. In the first verse of Ex. 17 it says, right after they pitched their tents, that there was no water for the people to drink! WOW. How do we reconcile that God is leading them from need to need? Again what is the first thing that comes out of the people when they realize they have the same need they had two steps ago? It says the people did "chide" with Moses. Moses retorted "why chide with me, don't you know what you are really doing is testing God?"

Herein is the crux of the matter. The people used every place of need as a test to measure God's provisional failure. They had the test backwards. They (we) have no right or basis to test God. In reality, God was testing them and their response to their need. They refused to look at their journey from His point of view. This reveals hardness of heart and unbelief in the people.

Chide means to grapple or wrestle with, or quarrel, or argue. Can't you just hear the people arguing with Moses, what is wrong with you? How did you get us here and not have any water waiting for us? Their arguments went on accusing him that he brought them to the wilderness to kill them by means of them dying of thirst.

Moses did what any sensible leader would do, he cried out to the Lord! "What should I do to this people they are ready to stone me?"

God said to Moses, "take the elders and your 'staff' that you used at the Red Sea and go to the rock in Horeb and strike it and water will come out of it and there will be enough for all."

Moses did this in the sight of the elders. Then he did a teaching to the elders. He called the place of the release of water by two names; Massah and Meribah, which mean testing and chiding. Moses was trying to tell the people they were missing the meaning of life. Every need they had they came to the conclusion that God failed them! The reality was that every need had a meaning that there was a new level of relationship that God wanted to make available to the people.

Moses closed the teaching with this question: "Is the Lord among us, or not?" The people's responses showed they doubted that the Lord was with them. Sometimes a question has more impact than a statement. It forces us to answer rather than passively agree or disagree. Elders walked away from that rock having to decide whether the Lord was with them or not.

Had not the Lord already proved that He could provide them water? Why not have a praise service and give thanks to God for His greatness? Why not sing to Him with thanksgiving, believing that He has a provision this time just as He had a provision for them the last time? If the Lord is with us surely we can trust that He knows and will provide! Maybe we need to come to grips with this question ourselves – is the Lord with me or not?

The training at Rephidim was not done. It was here that the very first outside human threat after the Egyptians, attacked the children of Israel. When the army from Amalek came, Moses told Joshua, "Go and choose out some men and go fight tomorrow." Moses further said, "I will stand on the hill and direct the army to counter the tactics of the enemy."

When the battle started, Moses and Aaron and Hur went to the top of the hill. When Moses held up his hand Israel prevailed and when it went down Amalek prevailed. Moses' arms got tired and Aaron and Hur had to help support those arms until the victory was secure.

Several important things happened here worth noting. **One,** God began to show the level of authority that He had put in the hands of Moses. At the same time, He showed the frailty of human authority by showing that man needed help from other men. Human authority can be very confusing to us sometimes. Often we want to see their failings and shortcomings and magnify them. But here we see we should do as Aaron and Hur and strengthen the hands of our leaders, not sit back and mock their weakness. Often we want to show human weakness in leaders to excuse our own weaknesses. If our parents do something wrong in moderation often we will do those same things in excess. Using them as our excuse and avoiding responsibility for our own actions.

Secondly, the Lord told Moses to write the words in a book. The significance here is there has always been argument about the availability of book writing at this point in history. So this command dispels that notion. Anyway, the Lord says I want you to record the fact that the day will come when I will eliminate Amalek and the memory of Amalek from off the earth. He made the point to write this down for Joshua's sake. We can see that God was grooming Joshua for a position in the future. He also was prophesying through Moses to the children that when the word came true in the future that they would remember that it was the Word of the Lord being fulfilled.

The **third** point came that Moses built an altar to commemorate a new and very key revelation of the Lord. He built the altar and called it Jehovah-Nissi. The Lord is our Banner. This name represents an understanding that the Lord fights our battles. The Lord will wage war against our enemies. He will lead in the battle. He will pave the way to victory. Moses knew there was not magic in his arms, that when he held them up it was a delegated authority from Jehovah-Nissi. That Moses and his arms were the sign of the Lord's involvement in power and authority.

Moses was declaring the revelation that it was the Lord strong and mighty that waged and won the battle of the day. It should have shown the people how the Lord works with His people. The significance here is great because in order for the children of Israel to take the Promised Land they would have to fight many battles. There were at least thirty three kingdoms in residence in the Promised Land and each one would have to be conquered. The people were being given an opportunity to learn how to work with the Lord in battle. Moses declared to the people that with His banner over the people that victory was certain.

The significance of the lesson was lost on the people. God's plan was for this to be a stepping stone to greater victories. The enemy in this case was not insurmountable, but the lesson was to begin to plant victory in the hearts of the people. The thinking was to go this way. The Lord was with me when I killed the bear. The Lord was with me when I killed the lion. Surely the Lord will be with me when I face Goliath. This is how the Lord wants us to think. But if we wallow in our hurts and fears, doubt and unbelief will take over. We will come to the place that no victory in the past will mean anything in the future because fear will dominate our anticipation of what we are facing. It is amazing how we will be so caught up with asking how we ever got into this place of need that we will actually miss the provision He has for our every need.

We have heard much in the way of the concept of "spiritual warfare" in the last twenty years or so in the church. We have all these battle cries that declare how great we will be in battle. Now there is no doubt this life is inundated with battles. The scripture is clear (2 Cor.10:4,5), "*that the weapons of our warfare are not carnal but mighty in God to the pulling down of strongholds, casting down imaginations and every high thing that exalts itself against the knowledge of God and bringing into captivity every thought to the obedience of Christ.*"

Perhaps the number one battleground we must learn to fight on is the battle of the mind. That means that we must learn how to fight the thoughts of the mind before we go battle over cities. God was trying to teach the children of Israel how to walk with Him. In doing that He was getting them ready to conquer the Promised Land. To do that they had to learn how He thinks and how He looks at things. But they continually wanted to look at circumstances from their own perspective and how it affected them in the carnal realm.

If we look at the Book of Acts from the angle of "spiritual warfare," we will come away with a different perspective than we have today. In Acts 16:16-24, we find Paul and Silas going to Philippi and ministering the Gospel. They did not go into the city and start searching for the spiritual strongholds of the city. They were first compelled to go to the city by a vision Paul had received. When they got there they went to where the women of the city gathered water and preached. Lydia got saved and many others. Then they were in prayer and a woman with a spirit of divination began to follow them. She was a great distraction to the ministry, but Paul put up with it for many days! It seems finally he was "grieved" over the constant irritation, and finally turned around and called the demonic spirit out of the woman. It was a male spirit and definitely a stronghold over the city. When that spirit was cast out all of her masters that benefited financially from her spirit were upset.

This is not unlike places selling pornography, clubs, and drugs in our cities today. These are spiritually based strongholds in our cities and when the power of that spirit gets broken they will go out of business. Unfortunately, we try to wage these battles in the political realm and their defeat and eradication are slow coming if at all.

But in the Book of Acts the defeated purveyors of this wickedness had Paul and Silas arrested and put in jail. But Paul and Silas used their incarceration to praise and worship the Lord and the jailer got saved. Later a strong early church was born in this city.

Paul did not go to Philippi **looking** for a spirit over the city. He went there to preach the Gospel. He went there to pray. The spirit over the city found him; he did not find the evil spirit. Paul and Silas were walking in the Spirit of God preaching and praying, and they fought the battles in the spirit along the way.

We likewise must learn how to walk with Him. The optimal way to walk with Him includes learning how to walk in the Spirit. We must learn how to be led by the Spirit. We must learn how to war in the Spirit. It will not come by singing a few songs. It will come the old fashion way. It will come as we learn how to bring every thought into captivity. It will come as we learn to resist the devil. It will come as we learn to trust God for every need. It will come when we wage battle with the "sword" in our mouth, which is the Word of the Lord. The Church thinks it wants to fight and is ready to fight – but such is not the case. We are looking for examples of won battles and instead we are seeing so many examples of lost battles in America. But, not to fear, as God got the children of Israel ready in several months time, likewise He can get us ready in a very short time.

Are we allowing Him to get us ready? Are we bitter and grumbling at every **whY** in the road? Or do we believe Him at every **whY**? Are we fearful and complaining or are we trusting Him?

A great friend and great preacher of the Gospel named Moses Vegh, preached an important message a few years ago at a conference I attended. He said that when Saul's army was faced with the army of Goliath that for forty days the army of Israel went out and "pantomimed" war. They got all dressed up in battle garb and arrayed themselves as if they were going to fight that day, but in reality they were afraid to fight. They looked like they were ready to fight. They talked like they were ready to fight. They got in position to fight. But they would not fight. Maybe we are in the same place today. On Sunday morning we look like we are ready, we talk like we are ready, we sing like we are ready, but we are not ready.

But God is getting us ready. Not the way we think. He will not need much time. All He will need is a willing people who will believe in Him. All He needs is a people that will go and do and say what He says to go and do and say.

There was another "life lesson" in the Wilderness of Rephidim. Evidently at the start of the journey, Moses had sent his wife and two sons back to her homeland to be with her family. Now, his father-in-law had sent messengers and brought Moses' family back to him. There reunion was a special time and Moses used it to rehearse to Jethro all the wonderful things the Lord had done for the children from deliverance out of Egypt up to the provision of water and food. Jethro was so taken with the testimony that he made offerings to the Lord. Surly this was a sign of conversion to acknowledging the God of the Children of Israel as the true God.

Then Jethro observed the management style of Moses. The people would line up to bring to Moses disputes that needed judgment from someone in authority. Moses was doing that from morning to night. It was hard on the people waiting in line and hard on Moses to sit there all day. Jethro said it was too hard and would wear both Moses and the people out. Jethro introduced the first governmental structure to the people of God. It was the first time in scripture that the people of God would be enlisted to participate in their own government.

Jethro proposed to Moses a **job description for Moses**. It was highlighted by three main functions. **First, Moses was to represent the people to God**. He was to be oriented in the priestly role of bringing to the Lord the needs of the people. He was to look out for the needs of the people and bring to the Lord those needs. To do this he would need to stay tuned into the people and be aware of where they were in their hearts and minds. **Secondly, Moses was to teach the people the laws and ordinances of the Lord and how they should walk before the Lord.** This included that Moses was to teach the people the kind of work that they were to do as required by the Lord. **Thirdly, Moses was to gather out from among the people male leaders** with the following qualifications: able men that feared God, men of truth that hate covetousness, and find men that would lead various group sizes from thousands, hundreds, fifties, down to tens. The job description of these rulers was to provide decision making to the lives of the people. They were to judge all matters that came up in the normal course of life and only the most difficult were then to be brought to Moses.

One of the problems continually facing the Church is the controversy over governmental issues. Since the New Testament speaks primarily of qualifications and call and very little on method and structures it is not our intent to solve that here. For this stage of the journey though it was evident that the Lord wanted to begin to introduce the idea of involving others in many of the everyday needs of government. In reading the text, first Jethro made sacrificial offerings to the Lord. Then he also told Moses in Exodus 18:23 that Moses should do this if the Lord commands you to do it. In other words verify that this counsel is pleasing to the Lord.

This step then was to further establish the reality that it was the Lord who was leading them, it was the Lord that was providing their basic needs of food and water, and it was the Lord who was releasing others into places to serve the people in governmental responsibilities. Keep in mind that this government was not of a spiritual nature. There was a government in the spiritual realm that was going to come at a later time. The sole purpose of this government body was to render justice that could not be handled in the family where most disputes were previously handled. Probably most issues that came up were between families and it was difficult to settle those issues without someone outside with proper authority.

SCRIPTURES USED FOR THIS CHAPTER

EXODUS 17:8-16 Now Amalek came and fought with Israel in Rephidim. And Moses said to Joshua, "Choose us some men and go out, fight with Amalek. Tomorrow I will stand on the top of the hill with the rod of God in my hand." So Joshua did as Moses said to him, and fought with Amalek. And Moses, Aaron, and Hur went up to the top of the hill. And so it was, when Moses held up his hand, that Israel prevailed; and when he let down his hand, Amalek prevailed. But Moses' hands BECAME heavy; so they took a stone and put IT under him, and he sat on it. And Aaron and Hur supported his hands, one on one side, and the other on the other side; and his hands were steady until the going down of the sun. So Joshua defeated Amalek and his people with the edge of the sword.

Then the LORD said to Moses, "Write this FOR a memorial in the book and recount IT in the hearing of Joshua, that I will utterly blot out the remembrance of Amalek from under heaven." And Moses built an altar and called its name, The-LORD-Is-My-Banner; for he said, "Because the LORD has sworn: the LORD WILL HAVE war with Amalek from generation to generation."

EXODUS 18:1-27 And Jethro, the priest of Midian, Moses' father-in-law, heard of all that God had done for Moses and for Israel His people—that the LORD had brought Israel out of Egypt. Then Jethro, Moses' father-in-law, took Zipporah, Moses' wife, after he had sent her back, with her two sons, of whom the name of one WAS Gershom (for he said, "I have been a stranger in a foreign land") and the name of the other WAS Eliezer (for HE SAID, "The God of my father WAS my help, and delivered me from the sword of Pharaoh"); and Jethro, Moses' father-in-law, came with his sons and his wife to Moses in the wilderness, where he was encamped at the mountain of God. Now he had said to Moses, "I, your father-in-law Jethro, am coming to you with your wife and her two sons with her."

So Moses went out to meet his father-in-law, bowed down, and kissed him. And they asked each other about THEIR well-being, and they went into the tent. And Moses told his father-in-law all that the LORD had done to Pharaoh and to the Egyptians for Israel's sake, all the hardship that had come upon them on the way, and HOW the LORD had delivered them. Then Jethro rejoiced for all the good which the LORD had done for Israel, whom He had delivered out of the hand of the Egyptians. And Jethro said, "Blessed BE the LORD, who has delivered you out of the hand of the Egyptians and out of the hand of Pharaoh, AND who has delivered the people from under the hand of the Egyptians. Now I know that the LORD IS greater than all the gods; for in the very thing in which they behaved proudly, HE WAS above them." Then Jethro, Moses' father-in-law, took a burnt offering and OTHER sacrifices TO OFFER to God. And Aaron came with all the elders of Israel to eat bread with Moses' father-in-law before God.

And so it was, on the next day, that Moses sat to judge the people; and the people stood before Moses from morning until evening. So when Moses' father-in-law saw all that he did for the people, he said, "What IS this thing that you are doing for the people? Why do you alone sit, and all the people stand before you from morning until evening?"

And Moses said to his father-in-law, "Because the people come to me to inquire of God. When they have a difficulty, they come to me, and I judge between one and another; and I make known the statutes of God and His laws."

So Moses' father-in-law said to him, "The thing that you do IS not good. Both you and these people who ARE with you will surely wear yourselves out. For this thing IS too much for you; you are not able to perform it by yourself. Listen now to my voice; I will give you counsel, and God will be with you: Stand before God for the people, so that you may bring the difficulties to God. And you shall teach them the statutes and the laws, and show them the way in which they must walk and the work they must do. Moreover you shall select from all the people able men, such as fear God, men of truth, hating covetousness; and place SUCH over them TO BE rulers of thousands, rulers of hundreds, rulers of fifties, and rulers of tens. And let them judge the people at all times. Then it will be THAT every great matter they shall bring to you, but every small matter they themselves shall judge. So it will be easier for you, for they will bear THE BURDEN with you. If you do this thing, and God SO commands you, then you will be able to endure, and all this people will also go to their place in peace."

So Moses heeded the voice of his father-in-law and did all that he had said. And Moses chose able men out of all Israel, and made them heads over the people: rulers of thousands, rulers of hundreds, rulers of fifties, and rulers of tens. So they judged the people at all times; the hard cases they brought to Moses, but they judged every small case themselves.

Then Moses let his father-in-law depart, and he went his way to his own land.

Acts 16:16-31 Now it happened, as we went to prayer, that a certain slave girl possessed with a spirit of divination met us, who brought her masters much profit by fortune-telling. This girl followed Paul and us, and cried out, saying, "These men are the servants of the Most High God, who proclaim to us the way of salvation." And this she did for many days.

But Paul, greatly annoyed, turned and said to the spirit, "I command you in the name of Jesus Christ to come out of her." And he came out that very hour. But when her masters saw that their hope of profit was gone, they seized Paul and Silas and dragged *them* into the marketplace to the authorities.

And they brought them to the magistrates, and said, "These men, being Jews, exceedingly trouble our city; and they teach customs which are not lawful for us, being Romans, to receive or observe." Then the multitude rose up together against them; and the magistrates tore off their clothes and commanded *them* to be beaten with rods. And when they had laid many stripes on them, they threw *them* into prison, commanding the jailer to keep them securely. Having received such a charge, he put them into the inner prison and fastened their feet in the stocks.

The Philippian Jailer Saved

But at midnight Paul and Silas were praying and singing hymns to God, and the prisoners were listening to them. Suddenly there was a great earthquake, so that the foundations of the prison were shaken; and immediately all the doors were opened and everyone's chains were loosed. And the keeper of the prison, awaking from sleep and seeing the prison doors open, supposing the prisoners had fled, drew his sword and was about to kill himself. But Paul called with a loud voice, saying, "Do yourself no harm, for we are all here."

Then he called for a light, ran in, and fell down trembling before Paul and Silas. And he brought them out and said, "Sirs, what must I do to be saved?"

So they said, "Believe on the Lord Jesus Christ, and you will be saved, you and your household."

CHAPTER EIGHT

STEP 8

MT. SINAI –DECISION TIME

Scripture Text: Exodus 19:1- 20:21; 24:4-18; 32:1-35 ; 33:1-23; 34:1-28; 40:34-38

The journey is now only in the third month from Egypt! That means between the sixtieth day and the ninetieth day that they arrived at the wilderness of Sinai. The orders from God were specific and clear so far, and this step was going to be a big one. As we go through this step it is important that we remember the Lord has used withholding as a means of drawing them closer to Him up until this time. The scripture is clear that He was testing them. A test in school reveals what we know.

This kind of life testing however was to show the people who they were, what they needed, and how to trust the Lord. He was proving Himself trustworthy and He was drawing them into relationship closer and closer. Remember the Lord was giving them everything they needed in due time in order to prosper them and help them find healing for their soul, and victory in living for Him. The people continued to resent the fact that God did not "seem" to be anticipating their needs. They did not want to have needs!

The Lord told them to set up camp at the base of the mountain and He told Moses that He wanted personal time with him on the mountain. If we will remember Moses anticipated this from the encounter at the burning bush when the Lord told him that they would meet again at "the mountain." Mt. Sinai was that mountain and here the Lord told Moses to tell the people the following key points: **1)** You saw what I did to the Egyptians and bare you on eagles' wings, **2)** I brought you to Myself, **3)** IF you will obey My voice and keep

My covenant you will be a special people to Me above all people, **4)** And you will be a kingdom of priests and an holy nation.

Moses came right back down the mountain and told the elders. They spread the word throughout the camp and the people were in agreement and said they would live up to their part. Moses ran back up the mountain and told the Lord that He had a deal! The Lord here interjected an interesting phrase. He said, "I would speak to you from a thick cloud so that the people would see and hear and then they will believe you when you talk from now on."

The Lord then instructed Moses to tell the people that there was to be a special meeting of all the parties in a couple days and that this was to be a very special time together with Him and the people. Tell everyone to wash their clothes, to avoid sexual contact, and to set aside the next couple of days in their heart and then on the third day the Lord would come down and be manifest to the people. The Lord also commanded that boundaries be set around the mountain, and told the people that whoever touched the border would surely be put to death. To further make the point He said man or beast would suffer the same fate. This was surely an important upcoming meeting and one in which the Lord was introducing parameters that carried grave consequences for breaking them.

Let us not miss the significance of this moment. We have assumed the people understood their relationship with God. Nothing could be farther from the truth. They had been slaves and had surely been confused about who God is as well as who they were. Over the past ninety days they were experiencing a newfound awareness of the living God. During this time they were beginning to take note of His power and interest in them. While the Lord was beginning to show them how great He is, He was now giving them the opportunity to recognize Him and receive Him as their Lord. They did this when they with "one voice" agreed to follow His voice and commands.

This was all going to be made official with the Lord on the third day coming up, in a ceremony that only God could put together. In other words there was a meeting of the minds between the people and God. The people had now made a decision – and that decision was to begin to follow God. Often we think they were already following Him. No, they were running away from Egypt! They had not, up until now, consciously made a rational decision to follow God.

The Lord planned a spectacular meeting that would be remembered throughout future generations. In Ex. 19:16 and further that dramatic meeting begins to unfold. The people were all gathered, the trumpet sounded long (an angel was playing!), there was thunder and lightning's, and a thick cloud with the loud trumpet. The moment was so dramatic that the people were afraid and actually trembled. Mt. Sinai was on smoke and the Lord descended upon it in fire. In fact the whole mountain quaked. The trumpet got louder and louder, and the Lord came down on top of the mountain and called Moses up to Him. God quickly warned Moses to tell the people not to touch the mountain or come close and Moses said they wouldn't. But the Lord sent him down again to warn them and to bring Aaron back with him.

The Lord then told to Moses and Aaron the Ten Commandments and the other ordinances that went with them. Unfortunately the people were so locked in fear and the drama of the moment that they wanted to end the meeting. They said to Moses that it was all right for him to talk to God but they didn't want to lest they die – there they were bound up in a death fear again. Moses interpreted the feelings of fear that rose up in the people again and immediately said – **fear not!** In essence he was telling them this fear they now had was not the old kind of fear. This fear at His Presence is a good healthy fear because it will keep you from sinning. Perhaps in today's church we are so worried about making God so accessible to people that we are leaving out the fear quotient. As we see such a rampant tolerance of sin maybe it is indicative of the lack of the fear of the Lord by His people.

Now during this time there was several comings and goings by Moses. He would go up the Mountain and talk with God and come back down and tell the people. Besides laws and such there were certain conditional promises God was making to the people. He began to tell them about what they would find when they got to the Promised Land. He told them there would be enemies but that their enemies were also His enemies and that His Angel would be with them and would cut off their enemies. He also warned them against bowing down to the gods of these enemies. He promised them that He would drive them out little by little. If He did it too fast the land would become desolate, but little by little, would be the best way to take over the blessings of the land. Isn't it funny how we naturally want victory swift and sure? God has reasons for it to go slow and sure. We often equate slow with unsure. Doubt seems to creep in when it takes time and the reality is the blessings will be greater when it goes slower.

After these back and forth forays between God and the people during which God laid out many conditions of the relationship and the promises that go with them, "the people with one voice committed that all the words which the Lord has said will we do!" Moses then wrote all the words of the Lord down in a book and built an altar with twelve pillars, one for each tribe. Moses then called for the young men to offer burnt offerings and peace offerings unto the Lord. Moses then took blood and he sprinkled it on the altar. He took the book called the book of the covenant, and read it to the people and they again said they were in agreement and they promised obedience. Then Moses took blood and sprinkled it on the people, and said the "blood of the covenant."

This was perhaps the most dramatic moment of the journey up to this point. Stop and think for a moment about the drama and power of the moment. This was not a Hollywood production. This was a setting orchestrated by the Living God with angels playing trumpets, smoke filling the air, earthquakes and thunder all as a background for the dramatization of the legal transaction whereby the parties (God and the people) were making mutual commitments.

The Lord of the universe had brought a people that had been in slavery for several generations and had chosen them to be set free and to leave against all odds. He was leading them to a place He had promised four hundred years earlier to their father Abraham. He was leading them through a desert and He was committed to care for them and heal them physically and emotionally. They had now at this point in the journey made a decision. That decision was, "we would do what you tell us to do. We will follow your rules for living. We will worship You and You only. You will be our God and we will be your people." This was sealed in blood. It was of the most serious nature. The blood of course exemplified death and unbreakable agreement. It was a solemn agreement, nothing casual about it. It was not something that could be changed or laid down at either party's convenience. It was a vow and was in all seriousness.

Moses then left the people and took seventy elders of the people and went back up the mountain. They saw the God of Israel, who is called this now to the people for the first time. He had been known as the Father of Abraham, Isaac, and Jacob but now He established the relationship with the people – **THE GOD OF ISRAEL!** Moses and the elders saw the Lord in a fashion that we can't quite translate into our understanding. The scripture says (Ex. 24:10) they were enabled to see into the heavenly realm and could see "the body of heaven clearly." Then the Lord said to Moses, "Come up to Me in the mount and I will give you tables of stone on which I have written the law and commandments that you will then teach to the people." What a moment, something written by God Himself in His own handwriting. Moses left the seventy elders and said that Aaron and Hur are in charge while he was gone. He then went up and a cloud covered the mount and the glory of the Lord covered it six days. On the seventh day God called Moses up even further on the mount and the sight of the glory of the Lord was like a devouring fire on the top of the mount in the eyes of the children. Moses went into the mount and he was there a total of forty days and forty nights

Often we think they got to Sinai and Moses went right up to get the Ten Commandments and everything was a secret. But notice that the people had entered into the covenant **before** Moses went to the mount for forty days. There had been high drama, the terms of the agreement had been laid out, and a decision had been made by each person individually and the entire population as a whole to follow the Lord. At this moment in time there was unity in the faith. There had been an actual shedding of blood and the agreement had been fully and legally sealed.

Now while Moses was on the mountain this time the Lord began to give him the pattern for the tabernacle or the meetings place where He would meet with the people on the earth in an official way and place. The pattern was given in great detail including not only the architectural plans but every decoration and utensil that would be used. In addition, the Lord spelled out the office of the priesthood, and the method of decision making using the Urim and Thummim. The Lord also spelled out the installation of priests and the promise that the Lord would dwell with His people.

Furthermore, the Lord spelled out ministry to be available to the people through the various utensils, and who the workers would be that would be called to build. Also they were to be reminded of the Sabbath and its importance as a sign between God and the people. Then the Lord gave him the two tables of stone that had been written by the finger of God.

Well. we know the story well, that at the same time that the finishing touches to the final agreement were being set between Moses and God that the people got very anxious. There is down through history evidence that something can come upon a people and stir a group of people to do things that are not the right things to do. There is a strength that comes in a collective agreement that will silence even the most sensible voice of opposition. **From the people's point of view Moses delayed coming down the mountain!**

We don't know exactly which day this took place but it might have been somewhere around thirty or so days after Moses had gone up. Remember the mountain was still in smoke, but they had received no news. The people of influence gathered around and came to a decision. They decided to go to

Aaron (who had been left in charge), and said to him to make them gods because we don't know or understand what happened to Moses.

Aaron said give me your gold earrings of all people and they did so. We know the story (Ex.32), and Aaron fashioned a golden calf. Upon seeing this calf the people proclaimed that this calf- a god of their own making - brought them out of Egypt. When Aaron saw that, he proclaimed that tomorrow would be a day of feast to the Lord – as in Lord of heaven. The next day the people gathered for a supposed feast to the Lord but ended up having a party of parties. They offered offerings and sat down to eat and to drink. But the next phrase said that they " rose up to play." Later it became evident that this meant that they engaged in debauchery and lewd activities. When Moses came back he saw them in their nakedness and drunkenness. As preposterous as this all seems to us as we look back at the events we need to learn from the examples here. It is too easy to say I would never do such a thing.

First let us see that the people, by worshipping the calf they were really worshipping themselves. They were taking credit for getting out of the land of Egypt on their own. Oh, sure God helped them, but didn't they do it after all? Conventional wisdom says that the Lord helps those that help themselves – doesn't He? In spite of the high drama of their agreement with God only days earlier there were more serious problems coming to the surface now. You can only blame your actions on slavery so long. There is no indication that the Lord in any way made an excuse for their behavior. He was not sympathetic; to the contrary He was livid with them. In fact, at the very moment of the party, God and Moses were in distraught conversation. Oddly we see the Lord express emotion that very few people can come to grips with. God told Moses to go back because the people "you" brought out have corrupted themselves. They have "quickly" broken our agreement made just days ago. They have already turned to other gods. Then God goes on to say to Moses that he should let Him alone, so that He can kill them and He will start all over with Moses and make a great nation out of him.

These are difficult words for us to read. Pause here, their rebellion stirred in God a desire to eliminate these people from off the face of the earth. In spite of the opportunities of reassurance and comfort and care the people quickly broke off from the Lord.

We are still in Step 8 of the journey and this, while being a key step for the people, also became a key step for Moses in his leadership. After God's expressed reaction to the rebellion, Moses stepped up to fulfill one of the most important needs of mankind – he became an intercessor. That is he took a position between God and the people. He became a bridge; he started to help the people even though they did not realize they needed help. He was taking a position with God on their behalf and they were still at a party and had no idea that he was representing them for their own good

How many times we are in error and at the wrong place at the wrong time only to find out later that someone was praying on our behalf at the exact same time! One of the mysteries of our present day faith is that Jesus is now our King and Lord. That while we await His return He is still ruling and reigning over the earth. The curious thing is His method of ruling. He rules by intercession, that is, He presently rules as a King by functioning as a Priest. Hebrews 7:25 says that He "ever liveth to make intercession for them (us)." It tells us in Hebrews 4 that He learned obedience through His suffering and that He has been tested in all the same things we have been tested in. We likewise have been tested in all the same things that the children of Israel have been tested in. It is that wonderful thing called life, in which God is looking for a people He can call by His name.

Life is a testing process for each person. The test is to reveal what is in us. Once whatever is there comes forth He is there to provide for every shortcoming, to make up for every deficiency, and to open His arms to relationship. It is hard for us to "see" that because we are so often trying to get through the trials and tribulations of life and are not quite sure what is going on. So God provides an intercessor. A bridge to God that we sometimes don't even realize we need.

Jesus' incarnation was the only wonderful way that we could ever find hope. God made Himself available to man by way of emptying Himself of His Divinity and coming in the same fashion that we are in (Phil.2). That is He imposed on himself the same limitations that you and I have. He then went through all the same testing that you and I endure. He was tested and proven while under the same limitations that you and I have. The difference was that He used every available resource that heaven had to offer. He knew the word of God and used it to fight His battles with the devil. He used prayer to find direction and what to do daily. He walked in the Holy Spirit, using the power of God for daily living and ministry. He received angelic ministry in both the wilderness of temptation and in the Garden of Gethsemane. These are the things the Lord has provided for our every need. And we have an intercessor always trying to bridge us to heaven and its resources so that we may be enabled to survive each test, burning away everything not of God in our lives, and purifying each of us.

Unfortunately, the children of Israel were now faced with a great flaw that could not be blamed on their past. It is evidently a human problem that transcends time, culture, politics, or economics. The Lord used the term "stiff-necked," meaning rebellious. We would think a slave would have a neck that is ready to go however it was pulled. But it is just the opposite. By the way we are all slaves and we all suffer with this same flaw. Before Christ comes into our lives we are all in bondage to sin. We do the things we don't want to do, we say things we don't want to say, and we go places we don't want to go. That is what a slave is. Until we are broken in and pliable to the leading of the Holy Spirit we continue to learn the lessons of being broken and challenged as to whether we will be available to God. This is what it means to be humble before God. That is we are available to Him for His use.

So here we are, while God and Moses were putting the finishing touches on this mutual commitment to each other, it is revealed that the people have a major problem of rebellion that surfaces as a result of a minor time delay of a few weeks of uncertainty. Because they did not quite understand what was going on with Moses, their true rebellious nature is quickly revealed. We like to assign blame or a cause for our reactions – whether they are good or bad. Can we hear the argument that says, "We would not have rebelled if you had not taken so long on that mountain. We did not know if you would ever come back down."

The truth of the matter is that sooner or later whatever is in our heart will surface. What brings it to the surface is actually irrelevant. What brings it to the surface is neither the cause nor the reason. What surfaces are things that are there in the inner person. Man looks on the outward appearance, but God looks at the heart. God is trying to bring to the surface in our lives everything that is there. It is too easy for us to live on the surface or outwards plane and not even know for ourselves what is "in there." The Bible says that the heart is deceitfully wicked and who can know it. The Lord wants to minister to our heart. The Lord wants to restore and heal our hearts. He brings to the surface not to hurt but to help. He is not off saying I told you so. He wants to show us how much we need him. We think our outer man has the needs when He is using the outer to show the inner – so that our inner might be saved and all that goes with salvation.

Moses approached intercession with reason in pleading the case with God. He reminded God of the great deliverance from Egypt and asked what would the Egyptians now say about God if He killed them? He then reminded God of His promises to Abraham, Isaac, and Israel.

Well the intercession of Moses had effect for then it says, **"The Lord changed His mind of the evil He thought to do to the people."** This is one of those mind boggling verses. Don't accept any convenient explanation or rationalization. Rather let us look at this evidence that clearly says **the Lord changed his mind**. The change came as a result of intercession. The intercession was not emotional but quite rational. The case was based on two key arguments: 1) what would others think of your Name, 2) remember your promise. It has been said the most effective prayers are those prayers that pray God's Word back to Him.

Now Moses went back down the mountain to the people, he secured their lives first, and I am sure he was thinking all the way down what he should do when he got there. We know what happened when he got back down there. Moses threw the tables of stone and broke them. His anger "waxed hot" and he talked with Aaron for a report after seeing them worship and dance naked before the golden calf. Aaron said he, "collected the gold and threw it in the fire and out came the calf!" Of course this was a lie. Then Moses stood at the gate of the camp and said, "Who is on the side of the Lord?" The sons of Levi gathered to Moses and he had them kill certain offenders. They killed that day 3,000 men. Moses then called all the people to immediately set themselves aside for the Lord. Moses on the next day said to the people that he would go back up to the Lord and make atonement for their sin.

He was continuing his role as intercessor. When he got back up the mount with God, he offered to God what only one other did in history. He said to God that their sin is great – they did in fact make a god of gold. He then asked God to forgive their sin. Moses then said to God that if you would not forgive them, then blot Moses' name out of the book. The ultimate intercession is a willingness to stand in for the one you are praying for. In fact, this is true intercession. Not merely to speak on behalf of the one in need. But to suffer in place of the one in need. We sometimes think that intercession is when we feel the pain in our heart for the one in need. But perhaps the highest form of intercession is to trade places literally with the one in need.

Moses evidently knew about the book that the Lord had. It is the Book of Life. Moses said erase my name from it. In other words, terminate my relationship with you, if that will allow you to restore your relationship with the people. Moses is demonstrating to us that sin is not a "say la vie." Oh well, no big deal, you shouldn't do it but it is water under the dam. Moses knew payment was required, a price needed to be paid. And he was offering his eternal life in payment for the sins of the people!

The Lord said no, that whoever sinned would be blotted out. The Lord said to Moses that, what He wanted done, was that Moses was to lead the people as originally planned. He again promised the Angel to go with them, and He also said that there would be a plague on the people because of the golden calf.

Then things got ugly between God and the people. He said he would give them the land flowing with milk and honey but that He would not go with them Personally. He threatened that He would end up killing them on the way because He knew their rebellion was not removed. Reality began to set in with the people and they mourned and they took off all their ornaments as the Lord instructed them and then He said He would decide what to do with them.

The next phase of this step was at once dramatic and memorable and more for leadership revelation than for people revelation. Moses set the "tabernacle" – the tent that was used for meeting with God - out on the edge of the camp and went to it and God came in the cloud. All the people witnessed the event. The Lord spoke to Moses, Friend to friend. Moses and God got very personal and spoke of their personal relationship. Moses said (Ex. 33:11-23), "you have told me to lead this people but I don't know who is going with me. You have also said that you know my name and that I have found grace in your sight and you consider these people your people."

God answered Moses and said, "My Presence will go with you and that I would give them rest." Then Moses asked for something very personal. He said, "Show me your glory?" The Lord hid Moses in the cleft of a rock and passed by him and covered him. This personal contact and ministry to Moses from the Personhood of the Lord is one of the epic moments for any man that ever walked the earth.

For the people this step finishes up with Moses being called back up the mountain to get two more tables of stone. This time Moses would have to do the writing. The Lord proclaimed, thus revealing another dimension of His goodness, that **"He is merciful and gracious and longsuffering and abundant in goodness and truth."** This brought to the people mercy and the principle of forgiveness. He proclaimed that He would forgive both sin and the tendency to sin. He also introduced again the concept of visiting the iniquity of the people to the third and fourth generation. Iniquity or the tendency toward sin was going to go with the people. They would have to deal with it through the family. Moses quickly pleaded with God to go with them. The Lord recommitted to the covenant and reminded them – no more idols. He declared to them that He is a Jealous God. At the same time and very importantly God was re-committing to the people that He would give them victory in the Promised Land. They had to again promise that they would not take up with the gods that were in that land, neither were they to inter-marry. The breach between God and the people was mended. It took a great act of intercession by Moses. It revealed the forgiving and loving nature of the Lord. It revealed the people had some inherent flaws that had nothing to do with past experiences, but that the Lord was willing to work with them anyway.

The Lord takes the covenant seriously, and when the people broke it, only an intercessor could bring the parties back together. In order for the people to come back they had to grasp the seriousness of their offense and the consequences that would come. So, God and His people came back together in re-commitment of relationship. God spelled out for Moses during another forty days of fasting on the mountain all the intricacies of the relationship, all the expectations on the people, all the methods of meetings that would take place between God and the people. And the journey then moves toward Step 9.

Surely virtually every one of us has at some time or another broken covenant with God. We are not talking about those that don't know God as **their** God. We are talking about those who have made a commitment to Him to follow His ways. While it is not something we can trifle with, it does happen. When it happens we can still find a hope. All is not lost. If we will return, if we will humble ourselves, if we will acknowledge our need, He is a merciful and forgiving God. Our God is gracious and longsuffering. Our Lord is abundant in goodness and truth. He is everything we need and more. If our tank is half full He will fill it up. God will always be for us what we need.

Maybe not always in the way or in the time we think He should, but we can always count on Him. We have the benefit of the One Intercessor who did give His Life for us. And His Life was accepted on our behalf. Therefore, we have a way back into covenant. This is not a license to go in and out whenever we want to. There are always consequences for our "fall aways" or our "backsliding." But the Word today is there is a way back. His name is Jesus. So many want to blame Him or others when they fall away from Him. Take the blame yourself, but come back – Today.

There is a time the scripture says He "winks" at our sin but after a time He calls us to task. None of us can understand that dimension of relationship with Him. We don't know when the time comes that He gives us up according to our ways and according to the fruit of our own doing. But it should be a fearful thing to us all. Can you imagine that God wanted to kill over two million people? It boggles our minds; it seems to go against how we have God packaged in the twenty first century western Church. I don't have the answer but maybe we just need to finally be willing to ask the question.

SCRIPTURES USED FOR THIS CHAPTER

EXODUS 19:1-25 In the third month after the children of Israel had gone out of the land of Egypt, on the same day, they came TO the Wilderness of Sinai. For they had departed from Rephidim, had come TO the Wilderness of Sinai, and camped in the wilderness. So Israel camped there before the mountain.

And Moses went up to God, and the LORD called to him from the mountain, saying, "Thus you shall say to the house of Jacob, and tell the children of Israel: 'You have seen what I did to the Egyptians, and HOW I bore you on eagles' wings and brought you to Myself. Now therefore, if you will indeed obey My voice and keep My covenant, then you shall be a special treasure to Me above all people; for all the earth IS Mine. And you shall be to Me a kingdom of priests and a holy nation.' These ARE the words which you shall speak to the children of Israel."

So Moses came and called for the elders of the people, and laid before them all these words which the LORD commanded him. Then all the people answered together and said, "All that the LORD has spoken we will do." So Moses brought back the words of the people to the LORD. And the LORD said to Moses, "Behold, I come to you in the thick cloud, that the people may hear when I speak with you, and believe you forever."

So Moses told the words of the people to the LORD.

Then the LORD said to Moses, "Go to the people and consecrate them today and tomorrow, and let them wash their clothes. And let them be ready for the third day. For on the third day the LORD will come down upon Mount Sinai in the sight of all the people. You shall set bounds for the people all around, saying, 'Take heed to yourselves THAT you do NOT go up to the mountain or touch its base. Whoever touches the mountain shall surely be put to death. Not a hand shall touch him, but he shall surely be stoned or shot WITH AN ARROW; whether man or beast, he shall not live.' When the trumpet sounds long, they shall come near the mountain."

So Moses went down from the mountain to the people and sanctified the people, and they washed their clothes. And he said to the people, "Be ready for the third day; do not come near YOUR wives."

Then it came to pass on the third day, in the morning, that there were thunderings and lightnings, and a thick cloud on the mountain; and the sound of the trumpet was very loud, so that smoke of a furnace, and the whole mountain quaked greatly. And when the blast of the trumpet sounded long and became louder and louder, Moses spoke, and God answered him by voice. Then the LORD came down upon Mount Sinai, on the top of the mountain. And the LORD called Moses to the top of the mountain, and Moses went up.

And the LORD said to Moses, "Go down and warn the people, lest they break through to gaze at the LORD, and many of them perish. Also let the priests who come near the LORD consecrate themselves, lest the LORD break out against them."

But Moses said to the LORD, "The people cannot come up to Mount Sinai; for You warned us, saying, 'Set bounds around the mountain and consecrate it.' "

Then the LORD said to him, "Away! Get down and then come up, you and Aaron with you. But do not let the priests and the people break through to come up to the LORD, lest He break out against them." So Moses went down to the people and spoke to them.

EXODUS 20:1-22 And God spoke all these words, saying:

"I AM the LORD your God, who brought you out of the land of Egypt, out of the house of bondage.

"You shall have no other gods before Me.

You shall not make for yourself a carved image—any likeness OF ANYTHING that IS in heaven above, or that IS in the earth beneath, or that IS in the water under the earth; you shall not bow down to them nor serve them. For I, the LORD your God, AM a jealous God, visiting the iniquity of the fathers upon the children to the third and fourth GENERATIONS of those who hate Me, but showing mercy to thousands, to those who love Me and keep My commandments.

"You shall not take the name of the LORD your God in vain, for the LORD will not hold HIM guiltless who takes His name in vain.

Remember the Sabbath day, to keep it holy. Six days you shall labor and do all your work, but the seventh day IS the Sabbath of the LORD your God. IN IT you shall do no work: you, nor your son, nor your daughter, nor your male servant, nor your female servant, nor your cattle, nor your stranger who IS within your gates. For IN six days the LORD made the heavens and the earth, the sea, and all that IS in them, and rested the seventh day. Therefore the LORD blessed the Sabbath day and hallowed it.

"Honor your father and your mother, that your days may be long upon the land which the LORD your God is giving you.

all the people who WERE in the camp trembled. And Moses brought the people out of the camp to meet with God, and they stood at the foot of the mountain. Now Mount Sinai WAS completely in smoke, because the LORD descended upon it in fire. Its smoke ascended like the

"You shall not murder.

"You shall not commit adultery.

You shall not steal.

You shall not bear false witness against your neighbor.

You shall not covet your neighbor's house; you shall not covet your neighbor's wife, nor his male servant, nor his female servant, nor his ox, nor his donkey, nor anything that IS your neighbor's."

The People Afraid of God's Presence

Now all the people witnessed the thunderings, the lightning flashes, the sound of the trumpet, and the mountain smoking; and when the people saw IT, they trembled and stood afar off. Then they said to Moses, "You speak with us, and we will hear; but let not God speak with us, lest we die."

And Moses said to the people, "Do not fear; for God has come to test you, and that His fear may be before you, so that you may not sin." So the people stood afar off, but Moses drew near the thick darkness where God WAS.

Then the LORD said to Moses, "Thus you shall say to the children of Israel: 'You have seen that I have talked with you from heaven.

EXODUS 24:3-18 So Moses came and told the people all the words of the LORD and all the judgments. And all the people answered with one voice and said, "All the words which the LORD has said we will do." And Moses wrote all the words of the LORD. And he rose early in the morning, and built an altar at the foot of the mountain, and twelve pillars according to the twelve tribes of Israel. Then he sent young men of the children of Israel, who offered burnt offerings and sacrificed peace offerings of oxen to the LORD. And Moses took half the blood and put IT in basins, and half the blood he sprinkled on the altar. Then he took the Book of the Covenant and read in the hearing of the people. And they said, "All that the LORD has said we will do, and be obedient." And Moses took the blood, sprinkled IT on the people, and said, "This is the blood of the covenant which the LORD has made with you according to all these words."

Then Moses went up, also Aaron, Nadab, and Abihu, and seventy of the elders of Israel, and they saw the God of Israel. And THERE WAS under His feet as it were a paved work of sapphire stone, and it was like the very heavens in ITS clarity. But on the nobles of the children of Israel He did not lay His hand. So they saw God, and they ate and drank.

Then the LORD said to Moses, "Come up to Me on the mountain and be there; and I will give you tablets of stone, and the law and commandments which I have written, that you may teach them."

So Moses arose with his assistant Joshua, and Moses went up to the mountain of God. And he said to the elders, "Wait here for us until we come back to you. Indeed, Aaron and Hur ARE with you. If any man has a difficulty, let him go to them." Then Moses went up into the mountain, and a cloud covered the mountain.

Now the glory of the LORD rested on Mount Sinai, and the cloud covered it six days. And on the seventh day He called to Moses out of the midst of the cloud. The sight of the glory of the LORD WAS like a consuming fire on the top of the mountain in the eyes of the children of Israel. So Moses went into the midst of the cloud and went up into the mountain. And Moses was on the mountain forty days and forty nights.

EXODUS 32:1-35 Now when the people saw that Moses delayed coming down from the mountain, the people gathered together to Aaron, and said to him, "Come, make us gods that shall go before us; for AS FOR this Moses, the man who brought us up out of the land of Egypt, we do not know what has become of him."

And Aaron said to them, "Break off the golden earrings which ARE in the ears of your wives, your sons, and your daughters, and bring THEM to me." So all the people broke off the golden earrings which WERE in their ears, and brought THEM to Aaron. And he received THE GOLD from their hand, and he fashioned it with an engraving tool, and made a molded calf.

Then they said, "This IS your god, O Israel, that brought you out of the land of Egypt!"

So when Aaron saw IT, he built an altar before it. And Aaron made a proclamation and said, "Tomorrow IS a feast to the LORD." Then they rose early on the next day, offered burnt offerings, and brought peace offerings; and the people sat down to eat and drink, and rose up to play.

And the LORD said to Moses, "Go, get down! For your people whom you brought out of the land of Egypt have corrupted THEMSELVES. They have turned aside quickly out of the way which I commanded them. They have made themselves a molded calf, and worshiped it and sacrificed to it, and said, 'This IS your god, O Israel, that brought you out of the land of Egypt!' " And the LORD said to Moses, "I have seen this people, and indeed it IS a stiff-necked people! Now therefore, let Me alone, that My wrath may burn hot against them and I may consume them. And I will make of you a great nation."

Then Moses pleaded with the LORD his God, and said: "LORD, why does Your wrath burn hot against Your people whom You have brought out of the land of Egypt with great power and with a mighty hand? Why should the Egyptians speak, and say, 'He brought them out to harm them, to kill them in the mountains, and to consume them from the face of the earth'? Turn from Your fierce wrath, and relent from this harm to Your people. Remember Abraham, Isaac, and Israel, Your servants, to whom You swore by Your own self, and said to them, 'I will multiply your descendants as the stars of heaven; and all this land that I have spoken of I give to your descendants, and they shall inherit IT forever.' " So the LORD relented from the harm which He said He would do to His people.

And Moses turned and went down from the mountain, and the two tablets of the Testimony WERE in his hand. The tablets WERE written on both sides; on the one SIDE and on the other they were written. Now the tablets WERE the work of God, and the writing WAS the writing of God engraved on the tablets.

And when Joshua heard the noise of the people as they shouted, he said to Moses, "THERE IS a noise of war in the camp."

But he said: "IT IS not the noise of the shout of victory, Nor the noise of the cry of defeat, BUT the sound of singing I hear."

So it was, as soon as he came near the camp, that he saw the calf AND the dancing. So Moses' anger became hot, and he cast the tablets out of his hands and broke them at the foot of the mountain. Then he took the calf which they had made, burned IT in the fire, and ground IT to powder; and he scattered IT on the water and made the children of Israel drink IT. And Moses said to Aaron, "What did this people do to you that you have brought SO great a sin upon them?"

So Aaron said, "Do not let the anger of my lord become hot. You know the people, that they ARE SET on evil. For they said to me, 'Make us gods that shall go before us; AS FOR this Moses, the man who brought us out of the land of Egypt, we do not know what has become of him.' And I said to them, 'Whoever has any gold, let them break IT off.' So they gave IT to me, and I cast it into the fire, and this calf came out."

Now when Moses saw that the people WERE unrestrained (for Aaron had not restrained them, to THEIR shame among their enemies), then Moses stood in the entrance of the camp, and said, "Whoever IS on the LORD's side—COME to me!" And all the sons of Levi gathered themselves together to him. And he said to them, "Thus says the LORD God of Israel: 'Let every man put his sword on his side, and go in and out from entrance to entrance throughout the camp, and let every man kill his brother, every man his companion, and every man his neighbor.' " So the sons of Levi did according to the word of Moses. And about three thousand men of the people fell that day. Then Moses said, "Consecrate yourselves today to the LORD, that He may bestow on you a blessing this day, for every man has opposed his son and his brother."

Now it came to pass on the next day that Moses said to the people, "You have committed a great sin. So now I will go up to the LORD; perhaps I can make atonement for your sin." Then Moses returned to the LORD and said, "Oh, these people have committed a great sin, and have made for themselves a god of gold! Yet now, if You will forgive their sin—but if not, I pray, blot me out of Your book which You have written."

And the LORD said to Moses, "Whoever has sinned against Me, I will blot him out of My book. Now therefore, go, lead the people to THE PLACE of which I have spoken to you. Behold, My Angel shall go before you. Nevertheless, in the day when I visit for punishment, I will visit punishment upon them for their sin."

So the LORD plagued the people because of what they did with the calf which Aaron made.

EXODUS 33:1-23 Then the LORD said to Moses, "Depart AND go up from here, you and the people whom you have brought out of the land of Egypt, to the land of which I swore to Abraham, Isaac, and Jacob, saying, 'To your descendants I will give it.' And I will send MY Angel before you, and I will drive out the Canaanite and the Amorite and the Hittite and the Perizzite and the Hivite and the Jebusite. GO UP to a land flowing with milk and honey; for I will not go up in your midst, lest I consume you on the way, for you ARE a stiff-necked people."

And when the people heard this bad news, they mourned, and no one put on his ornaments. For the LORD had said to Moses, "Say to the children of Israel, 'You ARE a stiff-necked people. I could come up into your midst in one moment and consume you. Now therefore, take off your ornaments, that I may know what to do to you.' "So the children of Israel stripped themselves of their ornaments by Mount Horeb.

Moses Meets with the LORD

Moses took his tent and pitched it outside the camp, far from the camp, and called it the tabernacle of meeting. And it came to pass THAT everyone who sought the LORD went out to the tabernacle of meeting which WAS outside the camp. So it was, whenever Moses went out to the tabernacle, THAT all the people rose, and each man stood AT his tent door and watched Moses until he had gone into the tabernacle. And it came to pass, when Moses entered the tabernacle, that the pillar of cloud descended and stood AT the door of the tabernacle, and THE LORD talked with Moses. All the people saw the pillar of cloud standing AT the tabernacle door, and all the people rose and worshiped, each man IN his tent door. So the LORD spoke to Moses face to face, as a man speaks to his friend. And he would return to the camp, but his servant Joshua the son of Nun, a young man, did not depart from the tabernacle.

The Promise of God's Presence

Then Moses said to the LORD, "See, You say to me, 'Bring up this people.' But You have not let me know whom You will send with me. Yet You have said, 'I know you by name, and you have also found grace in My sight.' Now therefore, I pray, if I have found grace in Your sight, show me now Your way, that I may know You and that I may find grace in Your sight. And consider that this nation IS Your people."

And He said, "My Presence will go WITH YOU, and I will give you rest."

Then he said to Him, "If Your Presence does not go WITH US, do not bring us up from here. For how then will it be known that Your people and I have found grace in Your sight, except You go with us? So we shall be separate, Your people and I, from all the people who ARE upon the face of the earth."

So the LORD said to Moses, "I will also do this thing that you have spoken; for you have found grace in My sight, and I know you by name."

And he said, "Please, show me Your glory."

Then He said, "I will make all My goodness pass before you, and I will proclaim the name of the LORD before you. I will be gracious to whom I will be gracious, and I will have compassion on whom I will have compassion." But He said, "You cannot see My face; for no man shall see Me, and live." And the LORD said, "Here is a place by Me, and you shall stand on the rock. So it shall be, while My glory passes by, that I will put you in the cleft of the rock, and will cover you with My hand while I pass by. Then I will take away My hand, and you shall see My back; but My face shall not be seen."

EXODUS 34:1-28 And the LORD said to Moses, "Cut two tablets of stone like the first ONES, and I will write on THESE tablets the words that were on the first tablets which you broke. So be ready in the morning, and come up in the morning to Mount Sinai, and present yourself to Me there on the top of the mountain. And no man shall come up with you, and let no man be seen throughout all the mountain; let neither flocks nor herds feed before that mountain."

So he cut two tablets of stone like the first ONES. Then Moses rose early in the morning and went up Mount Sinai, as the LORD had commanded him; and he took in his hand the two tablets of stone.

Now the LORD descended in the cloud and stood with him there, and proclaimed the name of the LORD. And the LORD passed before him and proclaimed, "The LORD, the LORD God, merciful and gracious, longsuffering, and abounding in goodness and truth, keeping mercy for thousands, forgiving iniquity and transgression and sin, by no means clearing THE GUILTY, visiting the iniquity of the fathers upon the children and the children's children to the third and the fourth generation."

So Moses made haste and bowed his head toward the earth, and worshiped. Then he said, "If now I have found grace in Your sight, O Lord, let my Lord, I pray, go among us, even though we ARE a stiff-necked people; and pardon our iniquity and our sin, and take us as Your inheritance."

And He said: "Behold, I make a covenant. Before all your people I will do marvels such as have not been done in all the earth, nor in any nation; and all the people among whom you ARE shall see the work of the LORD. For it IS an awesome thing that I will do with you. Observe what I command you this day. Behold, I am driving out from before you the Amorite and the Canaanite and the Hittite and the Perizzite and the Hivite and the Jebusite. Take heed to yourself, lest you make a covenant with the inhabitants of the land where you are going, lest it be a snare in your midst. But you shall destroy their altars, break their SACRED pillars, and cut down their wooden images (for you shall worship no other god, for the LORD, whose name IS Jealous, IS a jealous God), lest you make a covenant with the inhabitants of the land, and they play the harlot with their gods and make sacrifice to their gods, and ONE OF THEM invites you and you eat of his sacrifice, and you take of his daughters for your sons, and his daughters play the harlot with their gods and make your sons play the harlot with their gods.

"You shall make no molded gods for yourselves.

"The Feast of Unleavened Bread you shall keep. Seven days you shall eat unleavened bread, as I commanded you, in the appointed time of the month of Abib; for in the month of Abib you came out from Egypt.

"All that open the womb ARE Mine, and every male firstborn among your livestock, WHETHER ox or sheep. But the firstborn of a donkey you shall redeem with a lamb. And if you will not redeem HIM, then you shall break his neck. All the firstborn of your sons you shall redeem.

"And none shall appear before Me empty-handed.

"Six days you shall work, but on the seventh day you shall rest; in plowing time and in harvest you shall rest.

"And you shall observe the Feast of Weeks, of the firstfruits of wheat harvest, and the Feast of Ingathering at the year's end.

"Three times in the year all your men shall appear before the Lord, the LORD God of Israel. For I will cast out the nations before you and enlarge your borders; neither will any man covet your land when you go up to appear before the LORD your God three times in the year.

"You shall not offer the blood of My sacrifice with leaven, nor shall the sacrifice of the Feast of the Passover be left until morning.

"The first of the firstfruits of your land you shall bring to the house of the LORD your God. You shall not boil a young goat in its mother's milk."

Then the LORD said to Moses, "Write these words, for according to the tenor of these words I have made a covenant with you and with Israel." So he was there with the LORD forty days and forty nights; he neither ate bread nor drank water. And He wrote on the tablets the words of the covenant, the Ten Commandments.

EXODUS 40:34-38 Then the cloud covered the tabernacle of meeting, and the glory of the LORD filled the tabernacle. And Moses was not able to enter the tabernacle of meeting, because the cloud rested above it, and the glory of the LORD filled the tabernacle. Whenever the cloud was taken up from above the tabernacle, the children of Israel would go onward in all their journeys. But if the cloud was not taken up, then they did not journey till the day that it was taken up. For the cloud of the LORD WAS above the tabernacle by day, and fire was over it by night, in the sight of all the house of Israel, throughout all their journeys.

Hebrews 7:24-27 But He, because He continues forever, has an unchangeable priesthood. Therefore He is also able to save to the uttermost those who come to God through Him, since He always lives to make intercession for them.

For such a High Priest was fitting for us, *who is* holy, harmless, undefiled, separate from sinners, and has become higher than the heavens; who does not need daily, as those high priests, to offer up sacrifices, first for His own sins and then for the people's, for this He did once for all when He offered up Himself

CHAPTER NINE

STEP 9

TABERAH - AGAIN?

Scripture Text: Numbers 9:1; 10:1-10; 11:1-33

The month before the journey was to begin again; the Lord spoke to Moses and told him to let the children of Israel keep the Passover. This took place in the thirteenth month out from Egypt. The Passover was to have a powerful place of remembrance in the minds and hearts of Israel for time immemorial —**"Deliverance by the power of the blood."** This is the message for all humanity. Since we are no longer an agrarian society the talk of blood seems gross to us. But the fact of the matter is that our agreement with God requires the shedding of blood. Shed blood is the only acceptable payment for our sin. Shed blood of an innocent Lamb was the only acceptable sacrifice from which to supply the blood. God Himself supplied that Lamb; He is in fact that Lamb.

Well, the journey picks up again in Numbers 10:11 when it is time to take the next step. The timing is significant as always with God. This step started on the twentieth day of the fourteenth month. This means they stayed at Sinai for about eleven months. Sinai became the training ground as well as the receiving ground. **They received from God His promise that He is the God of Israel. They made commitment to God that they were His people.**

Now Moses was training them in all the requirements of the agreement. They had spent this time living with the law. It's funny how sometimes we think how horrible it was living under the law. That is a misconception. Before the law they had no standards of behavior. They did not know what was sin. They had no yardstick by which to evaluate where they were. They now knew what was expected of them as people and that can be a comfort. Remember that Jesus said He did not come to abolish the law He came to fulfill the law. The law is to us a schoolmaster to bring us to Christ. We are not under the law to justify ourselves, which can't be done. But the law serves to reveal the mind of God for our healthy living here on this Earth. We have often reduced the law to a behavior strategy. But the law is a strategy to reveal the heart. Sometimes we can do those things that look good on the outside but our heart is far from it.

Jesus said the sum of the law was love. First of all the law's basis is to love the Lord our God with all our heart and mind and soul. The second basis of the law is to love our neighbor as ourselves. He said this is the bottom line of the law. That was not a new teaching. That had always been God's intention. If we think about it, if we love God we will desire to do the first four commandments. If we love our neighbor we will desire to do the last six commandments. Our love for God and our neighbors should rule our behavior.

If we love God we won't have any gods before God, we will not make any graven images, we will not misuse His name, and we will remember the Sabbath day. These all speak of our vertical relationship with Him and provide us with the means of demonstrating our love for Him.

If we love our neighbor we will honor our mother and father, and we will not kill, nor commit adultery, nor steal, nor bear false witness, and we will not covet the things that belong to our neighbor. This is how we demonstrate our love of our neighbor. By our restraint in these areas we prove our love to God and people. Talk is cheap. It is easy to say "I love God, or I love you neighbor," but the proof is in the actions. Do my actions verify my statements? If you observed my behavior would you conclude that I love first God and then secondly love you?

As the journey began again there was a new sense of order. For the first time the names of each tribal leader were recorded. The cloud began to move and all Israel went in order to follow the cloud. Each leader brought a standard that represented the tribe and all followed the family standard. They went for three days following the cloud. When the ark of the Lord was carried forth Moses began a prayer that we implore today: "Rise up, Lord, and let thine enemies be scattered; and let them that hate thee flee before thee."

Consider the drama of the moment. Once I marched with thirty thousand Christians down the streets of my city with, singing, banners waving, and dancers were dancing, and all were praying together. I can imagine two million people, as far as the eye could see, walking in step together, knowing they are going where God is leading them!

At the height of one of the most magical moments in the history of mankind, an unbelievable thing happened. The people complained. The Lord heard it. His reaction was fierce. He was displeased and His anger was kindled; and the fire of the Lord burnt among them and consumed them on the uttermost parts of the camp. That is God killed those that were hanging on the edge of the camp, again unpleasant words to our Western mind. When you are on the edge that means that you are not all the way in – meaning you are not committed.

What could have been a time of unity and celebration and walking together in the Power of God was filled with complaint. We better get the picture quickly, God does not like murmurers and complainers and he will not put up with them. My sense in Numbers 11:1 is that God took the biggest offenders, those that were purposely lagging behind, and those that were on the fringes of the procession and killed them. He used fire to do it and the other people cried unto Moses and Moses prayed to the Lord and the fire was quenched.

He called the place Taberah: meaning "the fire of the Lord burnt among them." There were some people among them that were Egyptians that followed the Passover but were also willing to follow the Lord. At this time they began to lust. The children also began to weep and cried out who shall give us flesh to eat. They thought only of the fish they ate in Egypt and the cucumbers and melons and leeks and the onions and the garlic. They went on to say their "soul was dried away because all we have is manna!"

Both God and Moses became very upset with the people. Moses spoke up first, and asked God why he afflicted Moses with the charge to lead these people? He went on saying he did not birth these people yet God had laid the burden of them upon Moses. He went on that he could not provide flesh for these people and that the burden was too heavy for him (Moses). This is the cry of every leader at one time or another. All leaders can take comfort that Moses taught us how to cry out to God with a common leadership burden. Moses went so far as to ask God to just kill him. Moses' argument was profound; "If I have found favor in your sight you will kill me."

Before we see this as purely against the people see what Moses says next. "Let me not see **my wretchedness**." Moses was seeing what was coming to the surface in his own heart and realizing that **his own problems were being manifest** at the same time. God then told Moses to bring seventy men of the elders and that God would take the Spirit that was on Moses and give it to them. Then they would share the burden so that the "spiritual burden of the whole congregation" was not on Moses' shoulders alone.

Note the difference in reaction between the people and Moses. They cried out for something to fulfill their lust for different food. Their cry was demanding and filled with self pity. Moses cried out and asked for mercy. What came to the surface in his own heart was a recognition of his own wickedness and he offered to die because he saw how wretched his heart was. Notice then God provided help to Moses with others to share the burden that was becoming more than one person could handle. But to the people He gave them over to their lust.

Now the dynamic of the moment was precipitated by having to walk for three days and their resentment toward God's provision of food. God asked a powerful question and one that He would ask each of us sooner or later. "Is the Lord's hand too short?" The Lord will not tolerate any accusations against Him. He is good – good all the time. He is making sure that all things are working for good in our lives. To challenge God in His ability to help or provide for us is an insult of the highest order. It is demeaning to suggest that in some way God is not able. With God all things are possible. When something doesn't happen that we think should happen does not mean that God came up short. Either we didn't need it or He was testing us to see what would be revealed in our hearts in a time of need.

The wisest thing to do in a time of need is to look up and worship the Lord thy God with all thy heart and soul. A time of need is a time to thank Him for all His goodness. After all, the Bible says that all the silver and gold is His. He never runs out of money. He never runs out of solutions, He always has a way out. If we will set our heart on finding His way and believing we will find that way - then we will!

God had already flown in quail once before. It is not like He had never shown them He could provide. This time He flew in quail and they ate it until it came out of their nose! While the most gluttonous people were still eating, the wrath of the Lord was kindled against them and He smote them with a great plague. He then changed the name of that place and called it "Kibrothhataavah—meaning they buried the people that lusted." My friends God killed more people.

God has been quick to deal with the unbelievers and doubters of Him. Especially those that existed among the people that claimed to be in relationship with Him. He makes examples of the worst offenders to speak to the entire congregation. God has made it very clear that He will not tolerate complaining and murmuring. Notice that there is a difference between how Moses shared his pain with God and how the people expressed their pain. Moses showed no suspicion or accusation toward God as if God were not coming through for him. Compare that with the people who continually suspected and accused God.

What is being revealed is a continuing tendency of the people to refuse to accept what the Lord was doing in their lives. They would not get over the fact that He would not do things the way they wanted Him to do them. It says in Psalms that the Lord gave them flesh to eat but He also gave them leanness of soul. This means that in their own minds they were always missing something. They were short of contentment. When your soul is "lean" you are never satisfied. You never get enough. Life can be very frustrating with this kind of mindset. The scripture says, "We should be anxious for nothing, but in everything give thanks." Unfortunately the people were on a path of hardness of heart. At every **whY** in the road they came to, they continually had an accusation against God. Instead of accepting the **whY** as a test for them, and for the condition of their heart to be revealed, they took every **whY** as a test for God, and judged Him or His provided leadership for failure to do what they wanted or thought they needed done.

Just because we are hurting does not give us an excuse to sin against God. He still expects us to recognize who He is and how great He is. He does not say sin is okay based on our earlier life experiences. We are setting legal precedents from one end of this country to the other over excusing things like rape and murder because someone had terrible early life experiences. The truth before God is that we all must take responsibility for our own actions.

This step in the wilderness has brought to the forefront the increased displeasure from the Lord regarding their complaining and their appetites. Are we as a nation not struggling in these very same issues today? No matter how much things change, they stay the same. We as a nation believe we have a **right to always complain.** We think it is our right to always have another opinion how things should be done. The problem with this kind of thinking is that we don't seem to realize what we are saying to God. When we are complaining we are, in reality, telling God we disagree with what He is doing or the way He is doing it. God has made an allowance for appealing to Him in prayer. But, He has not made an allowance for us to complain or accuse Him of not taking care of us the proper way.

If the children of Israel had been given steak and potatoes every night they would have complained. It was not what they were given; it was what they were not given that generated the complaints. They were not given the luxury of ordering off the menu of Earth. Many a starving nation would love to get manna every day. Manna was the food that kept a nation of millions in good health for what ended up being forty years. Can you imagine eating that healthy for that long and complaining about it? But there was a lust that was not satisfied in manna. The "heart of the issue here" was they had a taste for something that wasn't satisfied by manna.

We as a nation are wallowing in our lusts these days. In our quest to satisfy our lust of the flesh and the lust of the eyes we are indulging in all manner of sin to try and appease those lusts. Unfortunately, we can never see or taste or feel or touch enough to satisfy those lusts. May God grant us forgiveness for our complaints and our lusting to satisfy the flesh?

SCRIPTURES USED FOR THIS CHAPTER

NUMBERS 9:1-5 Now the LORD spoke to Moses in the Wilderness of Sinai, in the first month of the second year after they had come out of the land of Egypt, saying: "Let the children of Israel keep the Passover at its appointed time. On the fourteenth day of this month, at twilight, you shall keep it at its appointed time. According to all its rites and ceremonies you shall keep it." So Moses told the children of Israel that they should keep the Passover. And they kept the Passover on the fourteenth day of the first month, at twilight, in the Wilderness of Sinai; according to all that the LORD commanded Moses, so the children of Israel did.

NUMBERS 10:1-10 And the LORD spoke to Moses, saying: "Make two silver trumpets for yourself; you shall make them of hammered work; you shall use them for calling the congregation and for directing the movement of the camps. When they blow both of them, all the congregation shall gather before you at the door of the tabernacle of meeting. But if they blow ONLY one, then the leaders, the heads of the divisions of Israel, shall gather to you. When you sound the advance, the camps that lie on the east side shall then begin their journey. When you sound the advance the second time, then the camps that lie on the south side shall begin their journey; they shall sound the call for them to begin their journeys. And when the assembly is to be gathered together, you shall blow, but not sound the advance. The sons of Aaron, the priests, shall blow the trumpets; and these shall be to you as an ordinance forever throughout your generations.

"When you go to war in your land against the enemy who oppresses you, then you shall sound an alarm with the trumpets, and you will be remembered before the LORD your God, and you will be saved from your enemies. Also in the day of your gladness, in your appointed feasts, and at the beginning of your months, you shall blow the trumpets over your burnt offerings and over the sacrifices of your peace offerings; and they shall be a memorial for you before your God: I AM the LORD your God."

NUMBERS 11:1-34 Now WHEN the people complained, it displeased the LORD; for the LORD heard IT, and His anger was aroused. So the fire of the LORD burned among them, and consumed SOME in the outskirts of the camp. Then the people cried out to Moses, and when Moses prayed to the LORD, the fire was quenched. So he called the name of the place Taberah, because the fire of the LORD had burned among them.

Now the mixed multitude who were among them yielded to intense craving; so the children of Israel also wept again and said: "Who will give us meat to eat? We remember the fish which we ate freely in Egypt, the cucumbers, the melons, the leeks, the onions, and the garlic; but now our whole being IS dried up; THERE IS nothing at all except this manna BEFORE our eyes!"

Now the manna WAS like coriander seed, and its color like the color of bdellium. The people went about and gathered IT, ground IT on millstones or beat IT in the mortar, cooked IT in pans, and made cakes of it; and its taste was like the taste of pastry prepared with oil. And when the dew fell on the camp in the night, the manna fell on it.

Then Moses heard the people weeping throughout their families, everyone at the door of his tent; and the anger of the LORD was greatly aroused; Moses also was displeased. So Moses said to the LORD, "Why have You afflicted Your servant? And why have I not found favor in Your sight, that You have laid the burden of all these people on me? Did I conceive all these people? Did I beget them, that You should say to me, 'Carry them in your bosom, as a guardian carries a nursing child,' to the land which You swore to their fathers? Where am I to get meat to give to all these people? For they weep all over me, saying, 'Give us meat, that we may eat.' I am not able to bear all these people alone, because the burden IS too heavy for me. If You treat me like this, please kill me here and now—if I have found favor in Your sight—and do not let me see my wretchedness!"

So the LORD said to Moses: "Gather to Me seventy men of the elders of Israel, whom you know to be the elders of the people and officers over them; bring them to the tabernacle of meeting, that they may stand there with you. Then I will come down and talk with you there. I will take of the Spirit that IS upon you and will put THE SAME upon them; and they shall bear the burden of the people with you, that you may not bear IT yourself alone. Then you shall say to the people, 'Consecrate yourselves for tomorrow, and you shall eat meat; for you have wept in the hearing of the LORD, saying, "Who will give us meat to eat? For IT WAS well with us in Egypt." Therefore the LORD will give you meat, and you shall eat. You shall eat, not one day, nor two days, nor five days, nor ten days, nor twenty days, but FOR a whole month, until it comes out of your nostrils and becomes loathsome to you, because you have despised the LORD who is among you, and have wept before Him, saying, "Why did we ever come up out of Egypt?" ' "

And Moses said, "The people whom I AM among ARE six hundred thousand men on foot; yet You have said, 'I will give them meat, that they may eat FOR a whole month.' Shall flocks and herds be slaughtered for them, to provide enough for them? Or shall all the fish of the sea be gathered together for them, to provide enough for them?" And the LORD said to Moses, "Has the LORD's arm been shortened? Now you shall see whether what I say will happen to you or not."

So Moses went out and told the people the words of the LORD, and he gathered the seventy men of the elders of the people and placed them around the tabernacle. Then the LORD came down in the cloud, and spoke to him, and took of the Spirit that WAS upon him, and placed THE SAME upon the seventy elders; and it happened, when the Spirit rested upon them, that they prophesied, although they never did SO again.

But two men had remained in the camp: the name of one WAS Eldad, and the name of the other Medad. And the Spirit rested upon them. Now they WERE among those listed, but who had not gone out to the tabernacle; yet they prophesied in the camp. And a young man ran and told Moses, and said, "Eldad and Medad are prophesying in the camp."

So Joshua the son of Nun, Moses' assistant, ONE of his choice men, answered and said, "Moses my lord, forbid them!"

Then Moses said to him, "Are you zealous for my sake? Oh, that all the LORD's people were prophets AND that the LORD would put His Spirit upon them!" And Moses returned to the camp, he and the elders of Israel.

Now a wind went out from the LORD, and it brought quail from the sea and left THEM fluttering near the camp, about a day's journey on this side and about a day's journey on the other side, all around the camp, and about two cubits above the surface of the ground. And the people stayed up all that day, all night, and all the next day, and gathered the quail (he who gathered least gathered ten homers); and they spread THEM out for themselves all around the camp. But while the meat WAS still between their teeth, before it was chewed, the wrath of the LORD was aroused against the people, and the LORD struck the people with a very great plague. So he called the name of that place Kibroth Hattaavah, because there they buried the people who had yielded to craving.

CHAPTER TEN

STEP 10

HAZEROTH - REBEL

Scripture Text: Numbers 11:35-12:16

Numbers 12 takes us to a chapter that reveals leadership principles that somehow we can seem to disassociate ourselves from, and not think they apply to us today. For a little background let us look at the players and their roles. Miriam and Aaron played unique roles in the Exodus. We know that Aaron was designated the spokesman on behalf of Moses. The chain of command was clear. God was the Commander-in-Chief and gave the orders. He gave them to Moses who was His choice for human leadership to direct the affairs of the people. And Moses was clearly the head. It was not a committee rule. It was God rule or theocratic rule.

God showed how theocratic rule worked. When He moved the cloud by day or the fire by night then, and only then the people were to move forward on their journey to the Promised Land. He orchestrated all events and these events were designed to show the people their needs and their dependence upon Him. He intended to continually reveal more and more of Himself so the people could draw closer to Him and receive His love. He would counsel with His human leadership and allow their input but He made all final decisions.

God spoke to Moses and Moses used Aaron as a messenger to get God's word out to the people. If we remember back at the "burning bush" Moses' fear was that he had some kind of speech problem. Moses felt it was a severe enough problem that he was using it as a major argument against God calling Moses to lead the people. But God had anticipated that and had already put it on Aaron's heart to go and find his brother Moses and offer to help him.

The order was clear. While Aaron had a prominent role it was not a role that carried with it the **directional authority** of the people. His role was that he was told what these directional decisions were and he then was responsible to convey them to the people. **He was a messenger not an initiator.** While a job description is not laid out beyond this charge to be the voice for Moses, we can grasp that the day to day requirements took him beyond that strict definition. For example, he would need to be able to speak to the people and then also answer their questions. The people would have access to Aaron and would question, probably daily, what does this mean or that mean? When and how would this directive be carried out? We can see that this could be a place where the people could begin to put their own interpretation on how far Aaron's authority went.

People are attracted to authority. They either want it for themselves or they want to be near it. They want to influence authority. If they can't get their own authority they want the next best thing and that is to have great influence over authority. Every person who has been second in command has had many pressures to move beyond the role of second in command and by whatever means, exercise authority that belongs only to the first in command.

The situation with Miriam was a little different. She was also a sibling to Moses. She had been the older sister who watched out for Moses when he had been placed in the ark as an infant, and Pharaoh's daughter found him to then raise him as her own child. When we first learn of Miriam on the journey she is leading a worship celebration (Exodus15: 20+). There it says she is a "prophetess." A prophetess is a woman who hears from God. At the same time, one who hears from God is to be available to share with others what God has spoken. It also says she took a timbrel in her hand and all the women went out "after" her. The implication is clear that she was looked to as a leader of women. What she did women following her then did the same things. We can be sure that women came to her everyday with questions and suggestions.

We learn that in Micah 6:4 it clearly says that God had sent the three of them to bring leadership to the people. It says there that He put the three of them "before" the people. So we have a good case that all three had leadership responsibilities. All three had a public position, meaning that the people saw them and recognized the three of them as leaders. They were to each carry out the functions as given them by God.

So what went wrong? In Numbers 12:1,2 we are told that Miriam and Aaron spoke against Moses. They had two accusations against Moses. First, they spoke against him because of the "Ethiopian woman whom he had married." When scripture is silent about the specifics of the case it is because their case was not the issue. In other words in God's eyes – the way God sees things – they did not have a valid reason to speak against the one God had designated as "the leader." Isn't it curious that this could have been a racial issue for certainly Moses' wife was black! Whether that was their issue or they did not like the way she did things, or did not like the influence that she had over matters of government we don't know for sure. The scripture does not say that she did anything wrong in her relationship with her husband or with God.

One thing we do know is that both Miriam and Aaron spoke against Moses. This implies that this had been discussed many times among them and that they came in agreement against Moses. Strength gathers in rebellion by back and forth verbal support. As the imagination works in discussions, weak points are dropped and points that have any support, even if only in the minds of the participants, gather strength and enable them to convince themselves that they have a good case.

Their second reason for speaking against Moses was very significant in its implications. They said, "Has the Lord indeed spoken only by Moses? Hath he not spoken also by us?" The very next sentence simply says that "The Lord heard." To our American way of thinking this at first sounds like it could be a legitimate question. Especially since we have already found in scripture that Miriam was a prophetess, which means she did hear from the Lord. So what is the problem?

The problem is the subtle problem that goes back to the Garden of Eden. If we remember the serpent said "Did God say.." It was not a question; rather it was questioning God's right to put such a restraint on Adam and Eve. But there is a difference between a question and questioning. A question has the purpose of seeking information not presently known to the one asking the question. That is it is for information purposes due to lack of knowledge. On the other hand questioning is subtle. As subtle as a two by four across the forehead! As in the garden, the purpose of questioning is to erode authority. The serpent knew what the Lord had said. His questioning was to undermine the legitimacy of the restraint in the mind of Eve.

"Has God said you shall not eat of every tree?" The serpent knew the answer so why ask the question? Only one reason and that was to bring doubt to the listener. Of course the question found a home. Adam and Eve had looked at that tree many times and thought about it and probably wondered about it. Well this time Eve looked at the forbidden tree again and thought in her mind that it looked very good. There had already been desire there and this questioning reinforced that desire and gave them an excuse to partake in eating the only restraint that God had put in their life. Mankind has suffered the consequences of that questioning "technique" every day since.

Behind "questioning" is an agenda. It is never to gain information but rather to gain a position. Sometimes a position is gained when someone else's position is diminished. Sometimes when those in authority lose some of their authority a vacuum is created that will rush to be filled by opponents. In the diminishing of authority by undermining tactics the vacuum is never filled by those sympathetic to the present leadership. It always goes to opponents or those with a different view. These are strong statements to make but as we will see there is a scriptural basis for this view. What we have come to accept as a right in the American way of life is actually sin. Our confusion is that judgment is not as swift as we will see in Number 12.

In verse 4 it says the Lord spoke "suddenly" to Moses and the other two. He asked them to come to the meeting place. The Lord then began to tell them the way it is. He went on to say "if" there is a prophet among you I will make myself known in a vision or a dream. It was as if He was telling them that He is the one that makes prophets and communicates to the prophet. The prophet's authority is restrained by the God given revelation. So, in essence He is telling Miriam that He has not invested her with directional authority. Her claim to fame is a support role of communication to the people of fulfilling God's agenda for the journey. Her role was clearly defined to support Moses under any and all discussions.

The Lord goes on to clarify His relationship with Moses. Moses, who is faithful (wow, imagine God assessing Moses as faithful!), and the Lord talks with him face to face. Their talks go beyond one Officer talking to another officer. Their communication is apparent, even for others to see. And Moses was given the privilege to see a representation of God Himself. God was declaring that while Moses had a governmental position he also had a personal position with the Lord.

God Himself then asks the question (questioning), "Because of this why were you not afraid to speak against Moses, my servant." Miriam and Aaron were making a fatal error in not looking at things how that God was looking at things. In other words, if God has put His stamp of approval on someone I better honor God's opinion. God is saying here who do you think you are questioning Moses? In reality to question Moses is to question God!

This point in the discussion between God and the three siblings can be disturbing to our twenty first century mindset. It can stir fear in us because if we apply it to today we might argue how do we know the man we are following in the faith is truly called by God as Moses was. What if we are under some charlatan's control?

First things first, Moses was clearly walking in the place God put him. Secondly, God is not telling us that we are not allowed to think when following a man of God. God provided checks and balances. We must make sure we are trusting God's ability to bring correction and direction. A clear example we have was when David at another time in history, was offered the opportunity to overthrow King Saul, certainly a king with lots of shortcomings. But David's view was "touch not God's anointed." This was also God's view; God would deal with King Saul in due time. It was not for David to pick that time. What complicated David's choice was that it almost looked like God had presented the opportunity to David to take matters into his own hands. But David was not moved by circumstances. He would only be moved by the will of the Father. Circumstances can be misleading. While God uses circumstances we must verify God's will prior to any action.

Miriam and Aaron could easily misinterpret the grumbling of the people that Moses must be doing something wrong. Surely if Moses were following the will of God the people would not always be complaining about Moses and the various decisions he was making? We have the advantage to look back at the account of the journey and see that the people were not a good judge of whether the leadership was walking in God's will or not. I wonder if anything is different today?

Can we imagine, since Miriam and Aaron were closer to the people than Moses that they were probably daily trying to explain to the questioning of the people the decisions being made by the Lord through Moses? Instead of being able to stand strong in faith believing that God knew what He was doing and that things were going to work for good, they allowed the people to wear down their own faith in God's purposes. It became evident that Miriam and Aaron began to buy into the complaints of the people. Probably there were people who kept telling them they should be leading and not Moses.

Let us remind ourselves that God was taking a group of slaves and in less than two years time He was training them how to conquer and rule in a Promised Land flowing with milk and honey. God knows what it takes to make that happen and the process is not a comfortable one. He was taking a slave mindset and converting it to a ruling mindset. He was taking a people that thought the good life was that your slave owner treated you well, giving you food and shelter and you did not have to work too hard. Whereas God had great plans for His people that they would learn to rule and reign in their own land. He planned they would be a people who would worship their loving heavenly Father - who would daily inspire them and show them how to walk in victorious living?

Maybe the American mindset is closer to the slave mindset than we would like to think. The American dream (mindset) is not much different than the slave mindset of home, job, food and comfort. But God has more likewise for us. He wants to teach us how to rule and reign in this life over all the bondages of life. He wants to bring a new freedom to His people that will allow us to go where He says to go, to do what He says to do, and to say what He says to say. To come to this place of ruling and reigning in life it takes the discovery of finding how to live in the will of our heavenly Father. This will entail not only the good but will also entail the difficult.

It will require us to live on a level beyond the desire for comfort in present circumstances. It will take us to a place that we will be able to accept that everything that is going on in life is working for the good in us. That all things that do come to the surface in our heart come at a time when God is there to heal or deliver. We come to a place to trust the living God in everything. We will see time and again that God hates complainers!

Regardless of what all was at work in motivating Aaron and Miriam - God intervened quickly and decisively. In what should be considered one of the most fearful things that could ever happen to any of us, the anger of the Lord was kindled against Aaron and Miriam. It says that God departed in anger (vs.9), and Miriam was left standing there covered in leprosy. Now Aaron took one look at Miriam and knew they were in trouble. Aaron then turned to Moses and said. "lay not the sin upon us; we have sinned and done foolishly." He went on and said, "let not her flesh be eaten away with this disease."

Moses had already been established in the role of intercessor. Without hesitation he began to intercede by crying out to God asking Him to heal her now. Moses held no grudge; he was not hurt over their words of insurrection so that he had to struggle to gather himself together to get himself to intercede. Moses was secure in his relationship with God and was able to function promptly. This moment is significant and gives the evidence that Moses had come to a place of revelation of the role and power of **"leadership intercession."** Every leader is faced with those times of leading people and for that matter leading other leaders, who are unable to see things from God's perspective. In our human experience these times can be a time of conflict.

Many a church split have taken place when this type situation has arisen. A great deal of confusion comes today when both sides to a conflict believe that God is on their side. Unfortunately God very seldom strikes someone today on the spot with leprosy. In some ways we almost wish He would in order to quickly clear up the conflict and settle who is right or wrong. But this apparent easy answer is not the answer, as we can learn from the ongoing journey of the children of Israel. For some time later another rebellion rose up and God judged them quickly by death—in fact He opened the earth and swallowed them up. But after that the people accused Moses of being the one who opened the earth! People have a great deal of difficulty seeing things as God sees things.

Leprosy is no longer a common disease. Likewise in the Church Age we seldom see God's immediate hand of judgment. Although I heard a firsthand account that in China during the "Cultural Revolution" that a Pastor was turned in to the authorities for preaching God's Word. During the trial the former parishioner who had turned against the Pastor was haranguing him while on the stand in a public square. Suddenly, with the square filled with townspeople, the witness turned with uplifted arm and he was struck with something like a bolt of lightning, although there was no storm or clouds. He immediately turned to stone and fell over. He actually broke apart when he fell and a hush fell on the crowd. Everyone got up and quietly went home and the trial was over!

Leprosy is a type or picture to us of sin. That means for us in the New Testament Church we must learn from this example, that given this role of supportive leadership function, we must not allow ourselves to be caught up in speaking against those God has put in authority over us. They obviously had not gone to Moses with their concerns. There are no discussions that are recorded that took place where they were seeking clarification. They had not tried to find how God was working in the situations that they were struggling to comprehend. There is no evidence they sought God or Moses. The evidence is that they had talked themselves into a justification of publicly speaking against Moses.

What we misunderstand today is that God's delay in apparent judgment does not mean that He feels any differently today toward insurrection by subordinate leaders. He still gets angry! Let us not mistake a delay as approval. There is no apparent justification for insurrection. Jesus said that if you judge another man's servant you are judging that servant's master. In other words, in this situation, to judge Moses was judging God. We might ask how is this? The answer seems to be that God is telling Miriam and Aaron as well as us today that He is able to deal with His servants in His own time and in His own way. He does not need our help.

As we look down through history we often see that God puts into leadership those leaders that reflect the condition of the hearts of the people. Often when history has judged a leader it was a judgment on the people that the leader was leading. In our own day the controversy with President Bill Clinton of the United States the focus had been on his shortcomings and failures and what to do about them. If we look at the Church's response during that eighteen month ordeal we can pretty well find the Church divided into two camps. One camp says we should forgive him and go on. The other camp wanted him ousted from the oval office immediately. Unfortunately we had no clear voice raise up to tell us what God was saying to this nation at that time.

The evidence strongly points to the fact that the President represents the nature and heart condition of the nation. We knew the kind of man he was and the struggles he had personally before he was elected. No one in this nation should have been surprised at his behavior; it was a lifelong pattern. Then what is God saying to us? In how many courtrooms this week did people lie under oath? Every trail attorney I have spoken to has said 100% of the courtrooms weekly have people who lie under oath. How many in this nation have committed adultery? While the statistics are not conclusive, if we take the scripture's definition of adultery as anyone looking on someone else and lusting after them, then they have committed adultery with them in their heart. Then maybe we are nearer one hundred percent for adultery than we want to admit. In any event, regardless of percentages, with the proliferation of pornography, and the amount and general acceptance of illicit sexual relationships that the percentage of Americans that participate in adultery is shocking and overwhelming.

What would God be saying? I propose the Word of the Lord to this nation is that we, the Church, must repent. Just because God tarries in striking us as a nation with leprosy does not mean He is ignoring what is happening. On the contrary, to whom much is given much is expected. What our President had done is a reflection of that which we have become as a people. Before we get too pious and deny our personal involvement in these type activities let us admit that these are national problems and pray God's forgiveness.

Whatever of these activities we are a part of in thought, word, or deed, please God forgive us. We are in a solemn time as a nation, yet we are eating and drinking and being merry, fooled by the prosperity we have enjoyed. The Church is not aware of the time or season we are in, may God help us to see this hour as He sees it. We are in a time where His goodness is leading us to repentance. We are misinterpreting the time as a time He is granting approval or ignoring our sin because He keeps blessing us as a nation. But let us remember that His blessings and gifting are without repentance. He blesses us for our giving nature as a nation. The blessings have nothing to do with any kind of ignoring of our sin that we are living in.

I have found it important to continually express my sorrow for my own degree of sin in this hour. May God grant us as a nation the gift of repentance?

Let's return to Miriam and Aaron and see what God did in their experience. Moses had interceded in prayer and God listened and made the decision. God told Moses that, "If her earthly father had merely spit in her face as a punishment for wrong doing that she would be an outcast for seven days." In other words, she would have been declared unclean and required to be separated from the people for seven days. So God said, "Send her outside the camp for seven days with no personal contact and then after seven days go ahead and let her back in the camp."

Now this *seems* like no big deal and why does it deserve an entire chapter of the Bible? Well, it is a big deal. It also says in scripture that during the entire seven days that the people could not journey forward. In other words, the judgment on Miriam affected the entire population of over two million people. Their forward progress was stymied for seven days. There is something else that happened that is difficult for us to grasp the significance.

In Numbers 20:1 it says Miriam died. The statement is actually no more than a clause in a sentence. In fact the next sentence goes back to another water crisis for the people. There were no eulogies spoken on behalf of Miriam. There was no time of mourning; there were no special burial provisions. There was no honor bestowed. She seems to be remembered in scripture for a song and a dance and not much more. Perhaps God's judgment on Miriam was much more severe than meets the eye – the human eye. Aaron, while again a participant, must not have been in the lead in the insurrection. He was not stricken with leprosy nor sent outside the camp. But he likewise died in the wilderness.

Before moving on let us consider one other verse with a key thought for us to grasp. Right after the accusations made against him, Moses was called a meek man, in fact meeker than any other man on earth (vs. 3). Often when we think of meek we think of mild mannered or gentle. But left there our understanding misses the significance of the quality. Let us consider the fact that Jesus called Himself meek (Matt. 11:29). He taught meekness in the Beatitudes (Matt. 5:5). As with all of the teachings of Jesus it is neither about mere outward behavior, nor only about relationships with people. But more significantly meekness is about an understanding of the grace of God in everyday living. It is that mindset and outlook on life that enables a person to accept all that life brings our way. It is a condition that a person who is meek is able to so trust God that they can trust and accept all of God's dealings and take comfort that they are all for good. And because they carry that outlook they take what comes without disputing or resisting.

A meek person believes God is in everything. So that while the journey was difficult, Moses believed God was in every step and therefore Moses walked in faith believing that. It was his reality. He was not always resisting God trying to get God to change how He was leading them every step of the way. He was humble, prayerful, and accepting. Imagine being called by God the meekest man on the entire face of the earth.

SCRIPTURES USED FOR THIS CHAPTER

Micah 6:4 For I brought you up from the land of Egypt, I redeemed you from the house of bondage; And I sent before you Moses, Aaron, and Miriam.

NUMBERS 11:35 From Kibroth Hattaavah the people moved to Hazeroth, and camped at Hazeroth.

NUMBERS 12:1-16 Then Miriam and Aaron spoke against Moses because of the Ethiopian woman whom he had married; for he had married an Ethiopian woman. So they said, "Has the LORD indeed spoken only through Moses? Has He not spoken through us also?" And the LORD heard IT. (Now the man Moses WAS very humble, more than all men who WERE on the face of the earth.)

Suddenly the LORD said to Moses, Aaron, and Miriam, "Come out, you three, to the tabernacle of meeting!" So the three came out. Then the LORD came down in the pillar of cloud and stood IN the door of the tabernacle, and called Aaron and Miriam. And they both went forward. Then He said, "Hear now My words: If there is a prophet among you, I, the LORD, make Myself known to him in a vision; I speak to him in a dream. Not so with My servant Moses; He IS faithful in all My house. I speak with him face to face, Even plainly, and not in dark sayings; And he sees the form of the LORD. Why then were you not afraid To speak against My servant Moses?"

So the anger of the LORD was aroused against them, and He departed. And when the cloud departed from above the tabernacle, suddenly Miriam BECAME leprous, as WHITE AS snow. Then Aaron turned toward Miriam, and there she was, a leper. So Aaron said to Moses, "Oh, my lord! Please do not lay THIS sin on us, in which we have done foolishly and in which we have sinned. Please do not let her be as one dead, whose flesh is half consumed when he comes out of his mother's womb!"

So Moses cried out to the LORD, saying, "Please heal her, O God, I pray!"

Then the LORD said to Moses, "If her father had but spit in her face, would she not be shamed seven days? Let her be shut out of the camp seven days, and afterward she may be received AGAIN." So Miriam was shut out of the camp seven days, and the people did not journey till Miriam was brought in AGAIN. And afterward the people moved from Hazeroth and camped in the Wilderness of Paran.

Matthew 5:5 Blessed *are* the meek, For they shall inherit the earth.

Matthew 11:28-30 Come to Me, all *you* who labor and are heavy laden, and I will give you rest. Take My yoke upon you and learn from Me, for I am gentle and lowly in heart, and you will find rest for your souls. For My yoke *is* easy and My burden is light."

CHAPTER ELEVEN

STEP 11

KADESH - READY?

Scripture Text: Numbers 13:1; 13:17- 14:39

We are now entering one of the most important steps in life that a generation ever faced. What the children of Israel did here at Kadesh not only decided their own fate. But what they did has had an impact on the people of Israel down to this day. But it is even more than that. Many a person, down through history, has done individually what they did here as a group. What happened here also reveals a very important understanding of the nature of our relationship with the Lord. It shows we do have a choice and it shows that **our choices can greatly affect the outcome of a matter**. How we respond to what comes to us in life greatly affects the outcome of our life.

Let's get things into perspective. The children of Israel have been on the road about fifteen months. The significance to this is that the Lord brought them by design, to the doorstep of the Promised Land, in an exact time frame from God's perspective. From God's point of view He had taken a group of slaves that had cried out to Him for help, and had given them all the help they needed.

In addition, God was fulfilling His promise to Abraham, that after four hundred years He would bring the children of Abraham back to the land He had given Abraham. While they had been on this fifteen month journey God was training them to be transformed from a slave mindset to a ruling mindset. Instead of thinking of life as a slave thinks, He was training them to think of life as a ruler thinks. To accomplish this He had put in their path on the journey certain pressures and roadblocks. The purpose of these **whYs** in the road were to reveal what was in their hearts. He did this not out of malice, but out of a heart to heal. It had been His plan to bring to the surface the hurts and pains of the slave life so that He might heal them. At the same time, He was showing them more and more of Himself. The more they would "know" of Him the more they would know how to rule and reign with Him.

When we know God as Savior, we can rely on His salvation and minister to others about His salvation. When we know God as Provider, we can rely on His provision and minister to others with His provision. When we know God as Almighty, we can rely on His power and minister in His power. When we know God as the "I AM," we can rely on the fact that He is always the same and can minister His unchangeableness to others. When we know God as forgiving, merciful, longsuffering, gracious, and abundant in goodness and truth, we can rely on these character qualities and minister them to others. When we know God as a Jealous God, we can rely on the fact that He is a God of total commitment and we can minister the fear of the Lord to others. When we know God as Leader and Ruler, we can rely on His Lordship and minister Him as Lord to others. When we know God as Healer, we can rely on His healing power and minister healing to others.

During these fifteen months the Lord revealed himself at least in these many ways and more. From God's point of view, the children of Israel were now healed enough and equipped enough, and knew enough about Him to go into the Promised Land. They were not ready any sooner, but He had done all that was necessary for them to be ready now.

So, this was the plan. God told Moses to send a representative from each tribe to go and "spy" out the land.

These twelve men were sent out with these instructions:

1) Go up on the mountain and look over the entire land,

2) Look at the people and see how many there are and how strong or weak they are,

3) See whether the land is good or bad,

4) Look at the cities and see if they live in tents or buildings,

5) See how the land produces crops and check out the forest for trees,

6) Be of good courage and bring us back some fruit.

The spies were gone for forty days and they returned with evidence of abundant fruit. Remember the children of Israel had not seen fruit for fifteen months and it took two men to carry one cluster of grapes. Listen to the report given by the majority: the land **surely** flows with milk and honey – **BUT** - the people are strong, the cities are walled, and there are even giants there. They even named some of the people groups there, as if "forget it; they are too much for us." They were **willing to forget** that the Lord on two different occasions told them an entire list of the present inhabitants of the Land, and that He would drive them out!

After fifteen months of training they were still **refusing** to look at things from God's point of view. This was no longer a case of needing more training; they had all the training they needed. **This was a case of hardness of heart and unbelief.** This was not a case of past hurts keeping them from going forward. This was a case that a healed people wanted to hold on to past hurts and failings. This was not a case of a people being thrown to the wolves by a cruel God. This was a case that a people would not include the power and love of their God into the analysis of life's circumstances. The majority report on the spy campaign left God out of the equation. They looked at the Promised Land from strictly a human perspective. They left out the God factor.

We are in a day when there is an exaltation of the "perceptions of the people." But God was not interested in the perceptions of the people. Any view other than God's view was wrong. God's strategy was not to meet the people where they were in their perceptions. He evidently did not feel the least bit obligated to try and cajole them out of their view. He did not acknowledge the validity of their wrong view. He was not willing to hold their hand until they came around to His "perception."

We know there was also a minority report. Caleb jumped up and grabbed the podium. A hush came over the crowd. Out of Caleb's mouth came these words, **"let us go up at once, and possess it; for we are well able to overcome it."** Can't we hear faith, hope, and confidence pouring out of Caleb's heart? Caleb believed God – period! The majority reporters jumped up in argument and said, "We are not able, for they are stronger than we are." Can't we hear their heart as well? They have chosen to look at the opportunity from a horizontal only viewpoint. The majority reporters then went into a counter argument based on fantasy, fear, and hardness of heart. To dramatize their point they went into exaggeration and fed on the fears of the rest of the people. This is an age-old technique for winning people to your side of an argument. Touch their fears or hurts and you can win a group to your opinion or to your agenda. Most political campaigns in America seek to touch on the fears of the people, to rally them to the candidate of choice.

The majority reporters actually said that the land "eats people." They then said that "all" the people were giants, and we were, "in our own sight as grasshoppers, and we are that way in their sight also." **These were two lies that revealed that they refused to look at things from God's point of view.** They admitted they were talking from their own point of view – "in their own eyes." Oddly enough we will see forty years later that how they said the enemies "saw the children of Israel" was also a lie. The majority report stirred the whole congregation. It says the people cried all night. If you will notice carefully they did not cry out to God for help, or for His direction, or for His Word to them. In times of fear or uncertainty these are legitimate things to cry out for. They just cried. Sometimes crying does not do us any good. They were claiming to be hurt and knowing that something bad would happen to them – which was not true.

Then the principle of mob rule kicked in, and the people began to murmur against Moses and Aaron! By just reading the scripture we can't see any justification for the outburst against human leadership – it was not like Moses and Aaron had anything to do with the present predicament. But the scripture says the "whole" congregation then said some things that were preposterous. They went back to their old reference point of accusing God of not letting them die in Egypt, and now they threw in the charge of "why did He not let them just die in the wilderness?" They then **challenged God** as to why He brought them to this Land, so they would die by the sword and that "our women and children" would be a prey to the inhabitants of the Land!

It is hard for me to comprehend these words as I read them. Yet, I have heard similar words over the last forty years. Words coming from people as if they have a right to accuse God or complain about God's leading of them. Many years ago I was faced with a difficult situation in my own life, and the thought came to me, "**whY** did this happen to me God?" And thought answer came right back to me, **"why not?"** Then I began to realize that if my life were examined, without the benefit of the shed blood of Jesus that whatever I was going through paled in comparison with what I deserved before a Holy God.

Thank God I have not gotten everything I deserve. Who placed me in charge with what was going to come my way in life? I cannot control my circumstances, nor can I control what is coming next. All I can control is how I respond to these things as they come my way. When bad things happen I need to put on heavenly glasses and see how God will be honored in my response to those bad things? The question always in these times of **whY** is this- am I willing to believe him? Or is my heart so hard and filled with unbelief that I won't believe?

In the case here, of the children of Israel, nothing bad had happened to them. They were told to check out the Promised Land and see what condition it was in and what the situation was. Then they were to come back and verify that the Land was everything God had promised. And that while the cities and people were strong hadn't God promised to go in with them? Their fears were stirred with the **threat** of difficulty. They relied on their old benchmarks for deciding how they would interpret what lay ahead for them.

Joshua and Caleb jumped back into the argument with the people. They challenged right back that the Land is wonderful and great. The Lord will bring us into it and will **give** it to us. The people looked at the Land and saw the problems and difficulties trying to go in there on their own. Joshua and Caleb were looking at the Land as a gift from God. When someone gives us something what do we have to do? We have to receive it. Sometimes that means we have to find out how to open the package the gift is coming in. The task of the children of Israel was **not how do "they conquer" the Land, but how do "they receive"** the Land the Lord was giving them.

The argument from Joshua and Caleb went further; they pleaded with the people don't rebel against the Lord, and don't fear the people of the Land. These are two key words that revealed the rebellious hearts and unfounded fears that rose to the surface. **There are some things that come to the surface that God brings up so that He can do something about them on our behalf. There are other things that come to the surface that we must come to grips with and deal with.** As in this case, only we can deal with rebellion and unfounded fear and hardness in our own heart. God's approved method for these things to be dealt with is that we are to admit our condition and repent. This means He expects us to recognize these sins and properly respond, with a humble heart toward him, asking for His forgiveness. But instead the people responded with shouts of "stone them, stone them."

Well, at this point God got involved into the fray. The glory of the Lord showed up over the tabernacle and before all the people. God did not talk to the people directly, thank goodness, for they would surely have died. **But God talked to Moses and made two key points: 1) How long will these people provoke me? 2) How long will it be before these people believe Me.** I have shown them all these signs all along the way, verifying that I am a Great God and their Deliverer, and yet they will not believe.

We may never quite grasp the significance of this moment in history. Each of us is faced with similar moments in life. I grew up in the day when the expression was, "When the going gets tough the tough get going." Well, that sounds quite macho and strong but it is human gobbledygook. For a Christian the real answer is; "When the going gets tough, we start believing God to show the way." It is a time to trust in Him. We are told not to lean on our own understanding. We are told to not trust in riches or the strong arm of the flesh. We are told to trust in the Arm of the Lord – his arm is not too short.

We seem to think that God's next reaction to the children of Israel is something He doesn't ever feel any more. In Numbers 14:12, God indicates He once again wants to kill them all, disinherit them, and start all over with Moses. Now remember this is a private conversation between God and Moses. The people know it is going on because they could see the cloud. But they do not know what is being said. The response of Moses is again at once startling and magnificent. Moses gets between God and the people and intercedes. He reminds God that the Egyptians will claim that God could not get those people into the Promised Land. And since He could not get them in He killed them! Moses then reminded God His Word to the people that spoke of the fact that the Lord is longsuffering, merciful, forgiving iniquity and sin. Moses then went further and pleaded with God that as serious as the sin has been would God in His mercy, pardon the people?

The Lord immediately responded and said, as you have asked I have pardoned according to your request. Then God chooses this time to speak a truth that transcends the moment. It is the Vision that God has for the end times Church. He declares that **"As truly as I live, all the Earth shall be filled with the glory of the Lord."** This declaration goes into the face of the concept of the premature rapture of the church. This Earth shall be filled with His glory and He will not leave it to another.

But, in the same breath God pronounces a judgment on the children of Israel. He said that because these people have seen all that I have showed them of my glory and my miracles and have still tested me ten times and have not responded to my voice, they will not see the Land. Joshua and Caleb, because they had "another spirit" and fully followed me, I will bring them into the Land. He wasn't done here. He told Moses and Aaron that, "Because the 'evil' congregation murmured against me I want you to turn them around tomorrow and go back to the wilderness. And in that wilderness, what you accused me of doing to the women and children I will do to you. Every man over twenty will die in the wilderness. Every woman and child that you have accused me of being willing to let die in the Promised Land I will in fact take them into the Land AND THEY WILL POSSESS IT."

There was one more judgment, and that was that their children would wander in the wilderness for forty years, one year for each day the spies were in the Promised Land. At that moment, the ten spies that brought the majority report were stricken with a plague and died immediately!

Whew, this is certainly one of the most heart wrenching confrontations between God and His people than at any time in history. It reveals a level of accountability for our responses to God that very few grasp the import of, in this day and age in the Church. The Bible does say "That vengeance is mine says the Lord." There is something in us that thinks that phrase is for someone else. But, rest assured there is a present day application that will have more meaning probably in the near future.

Let's get something very clear in our minds. The children of Israel were not turned away because they made a mistake. They were not turned away from the Promised Land because they had been afraid, or wanted water or meat, or even because they went to lewdness or worshipped a golden calf. The straw that broke the camel's back was that they lived the last fifteen months in a cumulative pattern of **choosing to not believe that God was able.**

They viewed each **whY** in the road as a failure on God's part. If you will, one of "nature's mistakes," which is a common present day expression. There was a pattern that they would not break – that God expected them to break – that doubted that God could or would provide for them at every turn. At each step God was there to reveal and to heal. Each step was to build their confidence and faith in the Living God. They used each step to blame God for the difficulties of life.

When Jesus ministered in Nazareth, He was only able to heal a few because they would not receive Him as the Healer and Savior. They had reduced Jesus to the limitation of being a carpenter's son. They refused the evidence of Messianic Personhood because Jesus did not put on the display that they wanted the Messiah to display. They refused Him. Jesus wept once over Jerusalem because they refused Him in their day of His visitation.

The children of Israel had an intercessor in Moses. We have a Great Intercessor in Christ Jesus. For the last two thousand years the Church has had someone bridging the gap between every failure and God. We have had an Advocate that continually pleads our case at every **whY** in the road. We have misinterpreted the grace and mercy as somehow reflecting that God has lowered His standards. Nothing could be farther from the truth. He is a Holy God. He is leading us and healing us and providing for us each step of the way.

He has shown us enough of himself for us to believe Him for the next step. How many of us fall short of His Promise to us because of unbelief? How many of us have not found our place in the Kingdom of God here on Earth because we would not believe him?

Many people don't like change yet that is what this life is all about. We are being changed from glory to glory. We are told in scripture to not be conformed to this world but be transformed by the renewing of our minds. The reason for this is so that we will prove what is that good, and acceptable, and perfect will of God. This requires change. This means that we are to cooperate with him as the One in our life who has begun a good work in us and He will complete it:

* When adversity strikes – **believe God**

* When we lose our job – **believe God**

*When death of a loved one comes – **believe God**

*When we don't know which way to go – **believe God**

*When His promise to us now seems out of reach – **believe God**

How can we please God? Believe that He is, and that He is a rewarder to those who diligently seek Him. The key is to let Him know we believe Him. There was an old Walter Matthau movie in which the character said at one point, "Do you believe your eyes or do you believe me?" A good question, can you hear the Lord saying it to you today? He doesn't care how strong or smart you are. He doesn't care how tall or how small you are. He doesn't care how rich or poor you are. He cares whether you will believe Him or not. **He has shown us that He doesn't use perfect people He makes perfect people.** Each of us is on our own journey. We are coming out of darkness into His marvelous Light. He has a place of Promise for each of us. As we travel along that path there will be **whYs** in the road. It doesn't matter if we stumble from time to time; it matters if we will believe that He will enable us to get up.

The scripture says that with God all things are possible. Do we just read that verse, but don't believe it, as demonstrated by the fact we can't walk in it? The believing is in the **whYs** in the road. Walk with him and believe him with all your heart. He will give victory if we will receive it!

We are not espousing a doctrine of merely positive thinking. What we are searching for is a proper outlook on life. We all need a revised way of thinking and looking at the circumstances that come our way in life. I have learned to ask some questions when I come to those **whYs** in the road. When circumstances seem overwhelming I immediately ask God for me to see Him in these dark moments. I have learned He is always there. I then ask what you are doing in these difficult moments Lord.

I can usually see what people are doing to me, or what problems are doing to me, but the challenge is what is the Lord doing IN ME? Now this can take some time to grasp. Our emotions often make it difficult to see or hear Him in those times. But we can take comfort in the fact that He will never leave us nor forsake us. Therefore, even though what He is doing may be difficult to grasp at the time, we can be assured that the day will come when it will become known to us. Then we will know that He was working for good in our lives, even in the midst of tragedy.

Immediately, my thoughts go to the seemingly untimely death of a loved one. Often, we ask how can that be for good. But, there is a verse that says in such a situation (Isaiah 57:1),"that none are considering that God knew what evil was coming their way and actually saved them from a life of misery." Another verse says that, "The death of His saints (or His children), are precious in the sight of the Lord." (Psalm 116:15).

God's ways are higher than our ways, and His thoughts are higher than our thoughts. Even when I have trouble trying to grasp what the Lord is doing in the midst of life's difficult circumstances, I can still believe Him. I can still trust Him. I can stand on the promise that all things work together for good. I can trust that while others may have meant it for evil against me, that God means it for good.

We can move forward to the place He is calling us to go. The bigger the road block the bigger the victory that will be ours through Christ Jesus. Adversity, threats, and accusations are common tools of the enemy looking to defeat us before we even get started.

Trust in the Lord your God. Lean not on your own understanding but keep your hearts and minds in Christ Jesus your Lord. There is an unfolding revelation that the Lord would bring to each of us. He wants to reveal to us much more than His Salvation. When His Lordship is manifested in our lives then we can walk humbly and yet with confidence that His arm is never too short. He is always able to reach out His hand to make a way where there is no way.

SCRIPTURES USED IN THIS CHAPTER

NUMBERS 13:1, 2 And the LORD spoke to Moses, saying, "Send men to spy out the land of Canaan, which I am giving to the children of Israel; from each tribe of their fathers you shall send a man, everyone a leader among them."

NUMBERS 13:17-33 Then Moses sent them to spy out the land of Canaan, and said to them, "Go up this WAY into the South, and go up to the mountains, and see what the land is like: whether the people who dwell in it ARE strong or weak, few or many; whether the land they dwell in IS good or bad; whether the cities they inhabit ARE like camps or strongholds; whether the land IS rich or poor; and whether there are forests there or not. Be of good courage. And bring some of the fruit of the land." Now the time WAS the season of the first ripe grapes.

So they went up and spied out the land from the Wilderness of Zin as far as Rehob, near the entrance of Hamath. And they went up through the South and came to Hebron; Ahiman, Sheshai, and Talmai, the descendants of Anak, WERE there. (Now Hebron was built seven years before Zoan in Egypt.) Then they came to the Valley of Eshcol, and there cut down a branch with one cluster of grapes; they carried it between two of them on a pole. THEY also BROUGHT some of the pomegranates and figs. The place was called the Valley of Eshcol, because of the cluster which the men of Israel cut down there. And they returned from spying out the land after forty days.

Now they departed and came back to Moses and Aaron and all the congregation of the children of Israel in the Wilderness of Paran, at Kadesh; they brought back word to them and to all the congregation, and showed them the fruit of the land. Then they told him, and said: "We went to the land where you sent us. It truly flows with milk and honey, and this IS its fruit. Nevertheless the people who dwell in the land ARE strong; the cities ARE fortified AND very large; moreover we saw the descendants of Anak there. The Amalekites dwell in the land of the South; the Hittites, the Jebusites, and the Amorites dwell in the mountains; and the Canaanites dwell by the sea and along the banks of the Jordan."

Then Caleb quieted the people before Moses, and said, "Let us go up at once and take possession, for we are well able to overcome it."

But the men who had gone up with him said, "We are not able to go up against the people, for they ARE stronger than we." And they gave the children of Israel a bad report of the land which they had spied out, saying, "The land through which we have gone as spies IS a land that devours its inhabitants, and all the people whom we saw in it ARE men of GREAT stature. There we saw the giants (the descendants of Anak came from the giants); and we were like grasshoppers in our own sight, and so we were in their sight."

NUMBERS 14:1-39 So all the congregation lifted up their voices and cried, and the people wept that night. And all the children of Israel complained against Moses and Aaron, and the whole congregation said to them, "If only we had died in the land of Egypt! Or if only we had died in this wilderness! Why has the LORD brought us to this land to fall by the sword, that our wives and children should become victims? Would it not be better for us to return to Egypt?" So they said to one another, "Let us select a leader and return to Egypt."

Then Moses and Aaron fell on their faces before all the assembly of the congregation of the children of Israel.

But Joshua the son of Nun and Caleb the son of Jephunneh, WHO WERE among those who had spied out the land, tore their clothes; and they spoke to all the congregation of the children of Israel, saying: "The land we passed through to spy out IS an exceedingly good land. If the LORD delights in us, then He will bring us into this land and give it to us, 'a land which flows with milk and honey.' Only do not rebel against the LORD, nor fear the people of the land, for they ARE our bread; their protection has departed from them, and the LORD IS with us. Do not fear them."

And all the congregation said to stone them with stones. Now the glory of the LORD appeared in the tabernacle of meeting before all the children of Israel.

Then the LORD said to Moses: "How long will these people reject Me? And how long will they not believe Me, with all the signs which I have performed among them? I will strike them with the pestilence and disinherit them, and I will make of you a nation greater and mightier than they."

And Moses said to the LORD: "Then the Egyptians will hear IT, for by Your might You brought these people up from among them, and they will tell IT to the inhabitants of this land. They have heard that You, LORD, ARE among these people; that You, LORD, are seen face to face and Your cloud stands above them, and You go before them in a pillar of cloud by day and in a pillar of fire by night. Now IF You kill these people as one man, then the nations which have heard of Your fame will speak, saying, 'Because the LORD was not able to bring this people to the land which He swore to give them, therefore He killed them in the wilderness.' And now, I pray, let the power of my Lord be great, just as You have spoken, saying, 'The LORD is longsuffering and abundant in mercy, forgiving iniquity and transgression; but He by no means clears THE GUILTY, visiting the iniquity of the fathers on the children to the third and fourth GENERATION.' Pardon the iniquity of this people, I pray, according to the greatness of Your mercy, just as You have forgiven this people, from Egypt even until now."

Then the LORD said: "I have pardoned, according to your word; but truly, as I live, all the earth shall be filled with the glory of the LORD— because all these men who have seen My glory and the signs which I did in Egypt and in the wilderness, and have put Me to the test now these ten times, and have not heeded My voice, they certainly shall not see the land of which I swore to their fathers, nor shall any of those who rejected Me see it. But My servant Caleb, because he has a different spirit in him and has followed Me fully, I will bring into the land where he went, and his descendants shall inherit it. Now the Amalekites and the Canaanites dwell in the valley; tomorrow turn and move out into the wilderness by the Way of the Red Sea."

And the LORD spoke to Moses and Aaron, saying, "How long SHALL I BEAR WITH this evil congregation who complain against Me? I have heard the complaints which the children of Israel make against Me. Say to them, 'As I live,' says the LORD, 'just as you have spoken in My hearing, so I will do to you: The carcasses of you who have complained against Me shall fall in this wilderness, all of you who were numbered, according to your entire number, from twenty years old and above. Except for Caleb the son of Jephunneh and Joshua the son of Nun, you shall by no means enter the land which I swore I would make you dwell in. But your little ones, whom you said would be victims, I will bring in, and they shall know the land which you have despised. But AS FOR you, your carcasses shall fall in this wilderness. And your sons shall be shepherds in the wilderness forty years, and bear the brunt of your infidelity, until your carcasses are consumed in the wilderness. According to the number of the days in which you spied out the land, forty days, for each day you shall bear your guilt one year, NAMELY forty years, and you shall know My rejection. I the LORD have spoken this. I will surely do so to all this evil congregation who are gathered together against Me. In this wilderness they shall be consumed, and there they shall die.' "

Now the men whom Moses sent to spy out the land, who returned and made all the congregation complain against him by bringing a bad report of the land, those very men who brought the evil report about the land, died by the plague before the LORD. But Joshua the son of Nun and Caleb the son of Jephunneh remained alive, of the men who went to spy out the land.

Then Moses told these words to all the children of Israel, and the people mourned greatly.

CHAPTER TWELVE

GOD'S WILL?

Scripture Text: Deuteronomy 1:1-3; 2 Chronicles 6:12-42

The book of Deuteronomy was written forty years and eleven months after the children of Israel began their journey! In this book Moses is rehearsing for the new generation all that the Lord had done on the journey over the previous forty years and how their fathers responded to Him. Moses also is telling them when they go into the Promised Land what the priorities are and how they should live their lives in order and faith before the Living God.

Before we get into what happened during these forty years, let's deal with something that has puzzled people since the dawn of history. Was it God's will that the children of Israel wander in the wilderness for over forty years? This is a big question because we all ask it from time to time about our own lives. Without compromise or confusion we can say **both yes and no**. First, was it God's will that they go into the Promised Land after Kadesh-Barnea? The answer is YES; it was God's will for them to go in about fifteen months after the start of the journey.

How do we know it was His will? He had taken them through eleven steps of revealing their hurts, healing their hurts, and revealing to them who He is and that He was their God and was able to fulfill every single promise He made to them. To God the twelfth step was to go in and take the land, believing that God was giving it to them.

Let us now factor in the responses of the people and the elements of the of the decision: a) the spies came back with a bad report, b) the people came to virtually a unanimous conclusion that it was too big a step, c) and they could not believe that even God could get them. Was it still God's will for them to go in after all this? The answer is NO; it was not God's will for them to go in!

Are we talking out of both sides of our mouth? No, what we are doing is learning a very important, little understood, principle about how God works with us and we work with Him. When they got to Kadesh, they were ready to go in and it was God's will for them to go in, because He was ready to take them in. But, **because they did not believe** they could make it and did not believe He would get them in successfully, God had to hold them back. The unbelief of the people hindered God's will. The language is tricky here. The unbelief of the people altered God's will. God does not force His will for our lives on us. He does not impose His will on His people.

All humanity has been given Free Will. That is, we have the choice to accept or reject what God has done for us or will do for us. When God says, okay it is time to go in to the place I promised. It is His will we go in. When we say no, because we don't believe, it then is no longer His will for us to go in. His will is changed by our response. His will carries with it conditions. It is His will for us to go in – only if we will believe He will take us in. If we don't believe, then His will is that we don't go in. God's will for our lives always carries conditions. God is the initiator of His will.

He will make known His will to His people as we walk out our lives. We are the responders to His initiatives. There is only one condition on our response – will we believe that what has been made known to us from Him is possible through Him? That means the choices in life are brought to us. He either brings them to us, or He allows them to be offered to us. He does not tempt us with evil, but He allows evil to be available. But how we respond to those choices is up to us.

Another way to grasp this principle is to realize that we have an interactive relationship with God. He initiates and we respond. Sometimes, in prayer, we take some initiative and He responds. But even in prayer there is an argument for understanding that He can inspire or take the initiative in us to be the cause or source of what we are praying. The interactive nature of our relationship requires that when He initiates something, like a promise, there are conditions He always places on the fulfillment.

A clear representation of the interactive nature of the relationship is spelled out in Solomon's dedication of the temple. It is in 2 Chronicles 6:12-42 (see below), and is laced with the conditional concepts that are worded like this: Lord if you do this and we do that then will you do such and such? This dedicatory prayer is filled with Solomon's understanding that the people will surely do wrong things but he prayed God's forgiveness when the people recognized their wrong and turned back to Him.

We must spend time with this thought, because it is so little grasped in this day and age. One of our big problems is we spend very little time thinking about the nature of our relationship with Him. God's will requires our faith to be active. If we will not believe, then Him forcing His will on us will not give glory to Him. He does not even force us to do good things that are against our own free will.

For the children of Israel, their **corporate negative response** to His known will caused for them to miss corporately the blessings of His will. Life was not all it could have been because of their hardness of heart and unbelief. As a result of an entire generation choosing to not go into the Promised Land then it was God's will for the children of Israel to wander in the wilderness for forty years. It was now God's will that all the men of war age (that is, twenty years old and older) would die in the wilderness. It was now God's will that the next generation be trained to go in and receive the Promised Land.

It was God's will to provide the cloud by day and the fire by night to protect and lead the children through the wilderness. It was God's will to be their every provision even though He sometimes withheld again to reveal things that were in their hearts and to reveal things about Himself. The wilderness continued to be their classroom. In reality, all of life is the classroom; we are being trained for Him and by Him. We have been created for His good pleasure. In this case the next generation was being prepared to take the place of the previous generation.

God requires that in order for us to find and walk in His will we must believe Him and trust Him. We must conclude that He will make every provision necessary for us to go into that place He has promised us. We must respond in a way that shows our confidence is in Him, that we believe that He will make a way even when we don't see a way. Jesus is the way, the truth and the life. No one comes to all the Father has for him any other way.

There has been a proposal on the Christian table to think of God's will from the standpoint of His permissive will as compared with His perfect will. That is one way to look at it. Here is another. God's planned (perfect?) will was that from Kadesh the children of Israel were to go into the Promised Land at the leading of the Lord. When they opposed God's planned will they were then faced with living in God's realized will. Their negative response of unbelief in Him disqualified them from enjoying God's planned will. To walk in His planned will they would have to believe Him every step of the way. God in His ongoing mercy and love then provided for them another route to take. They were reaping what they had sown. Thus their lives now functioned in the realized will of God. Their actual experience was still with God. He was still with them on a continual basis. While He had planned more for them, their sin kept them from that, so they realized His will for their lives on a lower level than He intended.

Often as a Christian we feel like there has been more for us than what we are experiencing. I look at my own life and know quite certainly that I am living in His realized will for my life. He had more planned for me, but at the age of eighteen I walked away from His revealed path. His faithfulness brought me back to Him some fifteen years later. While I have enjoyed much in my life and heart with Him I have been walking in His realized will for my life. This does not mean that life has lost meaning or that life is a failure.

Something to think about here is this. Today is the first day of the rest of your life. What you have said and done in the past is over. You can't take it back and you can't undo it. If we will humble ourselves and turn to Him, He will make the rest of our life meaningful as we learn to walk in His realized will for our life. We will still realize that He is Lord, we will better know Him, and our experience will still bear fruit. We can give Him glory and honor that is due His name. We can still be productive in the time remaining.

While we may have been able to build more or plant more had we not refused His promise on a timely basis, there is still work to be done. The harvest is white and the laborers are few. There is still work in the Kingdom of God here on Earth for willing hearts. For those of us who want to use the rest of our lives for His glory. For those of us who want to make the best of the rest of our lives, we can still find His realized will.

There was work to do in the wilderness, if they would just turn from their ways of hardness of heart and unbelief. May we find and realize His will.

Will we make the best of the rest?

SCRIPTURES USED FOR THIS CHAPTER

DEUTERONOMY 1:1-3 These ARE the words which Moses spoke to all Israel on this side of the Jordan in the wilderness, in the plain opposite Suph, between Paran, Tophel, Laban, Hazeroth, and Dizahab. IT IS eleven days' JOURNEY from Horeb by way of Mount Seir to Kadesh Barnea. Now it came to pass in the fortieth year, in the eleventh month, on the first DAY of the month, THAT Moses spoke to the children of Israel according to all that the LORD had given him as commandments to them,

2 CHRONICLES 6:12-42 Then SOLOMON stood before the altar of the LORD in the presence of all the assembly of Israel, and spread out his hands (for Solomon had made a bronze platform five cubits long, five cubits wide, and three cubits high, and had set it in the midst of the court; and he stood on it, knelt down on his knees before all the assembly of Israel, and spread out his hands toward heaven); and he said: "LORD God of Israel, THERE IS no God in heaven or on earth like You, who keep YOUR covenant and mercy with Your servants who walk before You with all their hearts. You have kept what You promised Your servant David my father; You have both spoken with Your mouth and fulfilled IT with Your hand, as IT IS this day. Therefore, LORD God of Israel, now keep what You promised Your servant David my father, saying, 'You shall not fail to have a man sit before Me on the throne of Israel, only if your sons take heed to their way, that they walk in My law as you have walked before Me.' And now, O LORD God of Israel, let Your word come true, which You have spoken to Your servant David.

"But will God indeed dwell with men on the earth? Behold, heaven and the heaven of heavens cannot contain You. How much less this temple which I have built! Yet regard the prayer of Your servant and his supplication, O LORD my God, and listen to the cry and the prayer which Your servant is praying before You: that Your eyes may be open toward this temple day and night, toward the place where YOU said YOU WOULD put Your name, that You may hear the prayer which Your servant makes toward this place. And may You hear the supplications of Your servant and of Your people Israel, when they pray toward this place. Hear from heaven Your dwelling place, and when You hear, forgive.

"If anyone sins against his neighbor, and is forced to take an oath, and comes AND takes an oath before Your altar in this temple, then hear from heaven, and act, and judge Your servants, bringing retribution on the wicked by bringing his way on his own head, and justifying the righteous by giving him according to his righteousness.

"Or if Your people Israel are defeated before an enemy because they have sinned against You, and return and confess Your name, and pray and make supplication before You in this temple, then hear from heaven and forgive the sin of Your people Israel, and bring them back to the land which You gave to them and their fathers.

"When the heavens are shut up and there is no rain because they have sinned against You, when they pray toward this place and confess Your name, and turn from their sin because You afflict them, then hear IN heaven, and forgive the sin of Your servants, Your people Israel, that You may teach them the good way in which they should walk; and send rain on Your land which You have given to Your people as an inheritance.

"When there is famine in the land, pestilence or blight or mildew, locusts or grasshoppers; when their enemies besiege them in the land of their cities; whatever plague or whatever sickness THERE IS; whatever prayer, whatever supplication is MADE by anyone, or by all Your people Israel, when each one knows his own burden and his own grief, and spreads out his hands to this temple: then hear from heaven Your dwelling place, and forgive, and give to everyone according to all his ways, whose heart You know (for You alone know the hearts of the sons of men), that they may fear You, to walk in Your ways as long as they live in the land which You gave to our fathers.

"Moreover, concerning a foreigner, who is not of Your people Israel, but has come from a far country for the sake of Your great name and Your mighty hand and Your outstretched arm, when they come and pray in this temple; then hear from heaven Your dwelling place, and do according to all for which the foreigner calls to You, that all peoples of the earth may know Your name and fear You, as DO Your people Israel, and that they may know that this temple which I have built is called by Your name.

"When Your people go out to battle against their enemies, wherever You send them, and when they pray to You toward this city which You have chosen and the temple which I have built for Your name, then hear from heaven their prayer and their supplication, and maintain their cause.

"When they sin against You (for THERE IS no one who does not sin), and You become angry with them and deliver them to the enemy, and they take them captive to a land far or near; YET when they come to themselves in the land where they were carried captive, and repent, and make supplication to You in the land of their captivity, saying, 'We have sinned, we have done wrong, and have committed wickedness'; and WHEN they return to You with all their heart and with all their soul in the land of their captivity, where they have been carried captive, and pray toward their land which You gave to their fathers, the city which You have chosen, and toward the temple which I have built for Your name: then hear from heaven Your dwelling place their prayer and their supplications, and maintain their cause, and forgive Your people who have sinned against You.

Now, my God, I pray, let Your eyes be open and LET Your ears BE attentive to the prayer MADE in this place. Now therefore, Arise, O LORD God, to Your resting place, You and the ark of Your strength. Let Your priests, O LORD God, be clothed with salvation, And let Your saints rejoice in goodness.

"O LORD God, do not turn away the face of Your Anointed; Remember the mercies of Your servant David."

CHAPTER THIRTEEN

WILDERNESS AGENDA

Scripture Text: Deuteronomy 8:1-6; Nehemiah 9:9-21

Well, we have left off with the children of Israel in between Step 11 and Step 12. It is worth our time to discover exactly what God was doing in this wilderness experience in and for the children of Israel. It will help us to find out what He does in and for us during these in between times that we also regularly experience. So much of life seems to be a transition experience. We often "feel" like God is going to do something new in our lives. There is often the sense that there is more to life than we are experiencing now, and often we are anticipating a change.

In order to gain understanding of what happened to the children of Israel in the wilderness we could discover that the most reliable interpretation of the Bible is the Bible itself. The Book of Deuteronomy interprets for us what was going on during the journey. As we said Deuteronomy was written after the fact. Often we have trouble understanding what is going on during various episodes of life. Very often it is not clear until after the fact.

I think it is very important that modern day Christians come to grips with one important truth as the Bible looks back over the forty years and eleven months of the wilderness journey. There is not one excuse offered for the wrong behavior of the people. Their slave experience is never offered as an excuse. At no time does scripture take pity on them for their slave life experience, as if it had something to do with their wrong responses to God while in the wilderness. We today are practicing many "inner healing" ministries in the church that often empathize with someone's background to the point of almost saying, "well no wonder you did that 'bad thing' look at what others did to you."

Regardless of their difficulties in life the Lord expected them to respond to Him and receive from Him all that they needed. The journey included healing along the way. God did not intend to memorialize their slavery. He wanted to memorialize the steps of deliverance. He wanted them to celebrate Passover, the Red Sea, and the other milestones of deliverance. He did not want to honor the hurt; He wanted to honor the healing. He did not want to honor times of defeat; He wanted to honor times of victory.

During the journey, the children of Israel were continually bent on going back to Egypt, but the Lord would never let them. The Red Sea experience was intended by God to be a Baptism, a separation from the past, a breaking from the power of the past. When we come to Christ and are baptized into Him, it carries with it a breaking from our own "Egypt." We have been delivered from the power of sin and death. We are to begin to walk in the realization and faith that regardless of what happened to us, or regardless of what we have done, we are now to begin to walk in faith and victory. In fact, Egypt is revealed as a " furnace" for the people. A furnace is always a place of purification when used in the Bible as a metaphor. Slavery was not a punishment but a purifier of Israel. This sounds harsh and cruel but it is not. It is the way of salvation.

God's purposes for the wilderness are clearly spelled out in:

<u>**Deuteronomy 8:1 -6**</u> *"Every commandment which I command you today you must be careful to observe, that you may live and multiply, and go in and possess the land of which the LORD swore to your fathers. And you shall remember that the LORD your* **God led you all the way these forty years in the wilderness, to humble you AND test you, to know what WAS in your heart, whether you would keep His commandments or not.** *So He humbled you, allowed you to hunger, and fed you with manna which you did not know nor did your fathers know, that He might make you know that man shall not live by bread alone; but man lives by every WORD that proceeds from the mouth of the LORD. Your garments did not wear out on you, nor did your foot swell these forty years. You should know in your heart that as a man chastens his son, SO the LORD your God chastens you. "Therefore you shall keep the commandments of the LORD your God, to walk in His ways and to fear Him.*

The **first purpose** was to humble the children of Israel. This strategy by God was not a negative. He was bringing them to the place to realize their need for Him. That is humbling. It is humbling for me to realize that I cannot save myself, that no matter what I do it is never good enough. It is humbling to know that I cannot find God on my own. It is humbling to know that the only reason I can love God is because He first loved me and gave His only begotten Son to die for me. It is humbling to know that He is superior and that I am inferior to Him. It is humbling to know that I can never measure up to His standards on my own, that without the shed blood of Jesus, I am doomed to everlasting damnation.

The **second purpose** of the wilderness experience was to prove or to test the people to know what was in their heart. What God was after here was to be able to show the people the meaning of the test: would they obey His commands or not? As we will see when they actually begin to go into the Promised Land, it was very important for them to obey Him. In order for them to find victory they must do what He tells them to do. Because what He tells us to do against one enemy will not be what He tells us to do against the next enemy. The only constant is Him, and from our standpoint our only constant is to obey Him.

The Bible here tells us that the reason for withholding food was to humble them. So what was unsettling and seemed very unfair at the time had a high purpose. It was also a teaching experience. In verse three it tells us that God was teaching man that man cannot live by bread alone, but by every word that proceeds from the Lord! Now we see that at the beginning of the ministry of Jesus on earth, that Jesus Himself had a wilderness experience. Jesus' self-imposed withholding of food for forty days in the wilderness was to demonstrate His humility and reliance on every Word that came from the Father's mouth. His victories over the devil's temptations in His own wilderness experience came from quoting this Word from Moses in Deuteronomy.

God's **third purpose** was that He used the wilderness as a means to chasten them as a father chastens his son. There was a teaching agenda behind that chastening. God wanted to train them to keep His commandments, to walk in His ways, and to fear Him. The Bible clearly tells us that His motive behind chastening is His love for us. In fact, His love requires Him to chasten us. He loves us so much that He will not leave us in the condition we are in. His chastening in our lives is always for our good. When we don't know what is going on in our life and times seem tough, we usually can look back at a later date and find that one or all of these three purposes were at work in us. Don't bother to go and challenge Him when we think enough is enough. He knows when that is – trust Him. The best thing to do during those in-between times is praise Him. When you are not sure of what is going on – worship Him with all your heart. No matter what it feels like He is not letting you down. You are not forgotten.

There are several places in the Bible where we are given insight into what was going on in the wilderness. They are not contradictory, but rather are further explanatory. In **Nehemiah 9:9-21** we are told that the people and the fathers of the tribes responded with pride and hardened their necks and they would not listen to the commands of God. It further says that they refused to obey and they disregarded the wonders that God did. In fact, their rebellion was so great that they even appointed a captain to go back to Egypt. Nehemiah goes on to say though that God was ready to pardon, that He is gracious, and merciful, and slow to anger, and would not forsake them. Nehemiah clearly taught that the Lord was right in His approach but that He had to deal with the people according to the condition of their heart.

How many times have we claimed that we feel like we are in a wilderness time in our life and are complaining that nothing is going on? The reality is that there is a lot going on, not outwardly but inwardly. If we will only look at the wilderness time from God's point of view, we will see that He is doing a great work. We like those works that show immediate, tangible, outward results. But He is after immediate, intangible, and inward works. It is from the inward work that our fruit will spring forth. You will find that every athlete will tell you they won the race when they were at practice. The results of the actual competition were based on the amount and quality of the work they engaged in when no one was looking. The disciplines in training bear fruit in the performance.

All too often we want the victory without the inner work. We want the fruit without the disciplines of the faith. If for example, we will not obey God over developing control over the lust of the flesh, how can we obey God when our enemy throws temptation in our path while we are on the road to victory? Often people in the midst of the wilderness want to throw in the towel because victory looks so far away. The promise seems so remote. That is the time to worship the Lord with all our heart. That is the time to not lean on our own understanding, but to keep our hearts and minds in Christ Jesus.

I have heard many people say that they must be in a wilderness time because they feel so " dry." We get dry only when we have allowed something to stop up the wells of life that are in us. Jesus said that if you ask me for a drink that you will never thirst again. In John 7:37-39 we are told that He was talking about the Holy Spirit that He would give to us. This means that when we are " dry" it is because we are not working with the Holy Spirit. That we are drifting off course, that we need the Holy Spirit to humble us, chasten us and turn us back to proper worship in faith of our heavenly Father. Dryness is not from a wilderness experience it is from a relational problem with our God.

Let's not forget that what happened to the children of Israel in the wilderness was an example for us. When I get honest with myself and honest with God I find that I must humble myself and admit how much I need Him in my life. My very survival depends on Him. When I accept that He is chastening me and not the people that seem to be against me, I can come to grips with the fact that His correction of me is because He loves me, and that He refuses to leave me in the condition He found me in. When I yield to His working and stand and trust Him and believe that He has everything in His care and that He knows what He is doing, I can find a peace that passes all understanding. The more I cooperate and believe in Him the closer I am to realizing His promises for my life.

Another important thing for us to grasp about the in between times, in this case forty years, is that the Lord had to train up a whole new generation of people. Obviously He had to break the negative influence the older generation had on the younger. He only had three male examples to put before them. They had to learn from a negative standpoint, by observing the consequences of the older generation's lack of faith. They learned what not to do rather than what to do. The point was clearly made to them that death comes from hardness of heart, rebellion and unbelief.

At the same time they were forced to learn to walk with God in the wilderness and not in the Promised Land. For example if you had been a ten-year-old at Kadesh-Barnea, you were not going to get into the "land flowing with milk and honey" until you were 50 years old! There are consequences to our sin of unbelief and hardness of heart that go beyond our own experience. We do affect our families and loved ones. The children and even the grand children were adversely affected by the sin of that first generation out of Egypt. The prime productive lives of hundreds of thousands of people were wasted in the wilderness. God's planned will was that by the time the book of Deuteronomy was written that the children would have been living in the Promised Land for forty years. They would have experienced the victory over their enemies. They would have enjoyed the fruit of the Land. They would be ruling and reigning with the Lord. They would have been walking in faith serving the Lord and keeping His commandments and developing their understanding of Him and their love for Him – and better understanding His love for them.

But God's realized will was that they had to walk in daily need for His provision. They were kept from productive lives. They could not plant anything. They could not grow anything. They could not build anything. They could not travel on their own. They were forced into close living conditions and tight living quarters. Tent living might seem fun for a weekend, but for forty years with a couple million others with their tents in close proximity is another story.

It was God's will all right for them to wander another forty years, but it was an expensive lesson to the next generation. But let us not forget He was there every step of the way. He covered them and protected them. He provided for them and cared for them and loved them. He worked with them and trained them. He got them ready to realize His will and make the best of the rest. Walking in the realized will of God is far superior than walking in our own will. The end of our own will is destruction. Our own will results in us being disqualified from even His realized will. That is the place where He turns His back to us. That is the place where we fully reap what we sow. Mercy leaves us and misery follows us.

Our own will, living independent of Him, has only one solution – Repentance. To repent means to turn around. Our own will means we are going in a different direction than what the Lord had intended. The means back is to turn from our own way and begin to walk in His way. His way is narrow and straight. A Christian must constantly look at their life and verify that they are walking according to His expressed will for their lives.

When we are in those in between times it is the best time to take stock of our relationship with Him. It is a time for adjustment and correction. When we come to these times we must learn to embrace them. We must learn to rejoice and be thankful. We have an opportunity to get back to the place He originally promised us. Other than those actually responsible for the sin at Kadesh, He still planned that the rest of them were to go into the Promised Land.

Maybe another way to think about this is to consider that the Lord is trying to figure out how to make us eligible to find His planned will. This is not said in the sense that He doesn't know. But if we would orient our thinking that the Lord always wants (wills!) that He bring to us whatever it takes for us to believe Him and desire to walk with Him in faith. His planned will for this people could still be experienced in the sense that the next generation would experience it but at a later age. Looking at the countless generations that were to follow, the long term planned will of God for the nation was still available to the progeny of Abraham.

The Bible says it is God's will that all would be saved. His will has therefore made Salvation available to all of mankind. Unfortunately not all will receive His Salvation. The key to our Salvation is not our works or what we can do or earn. The key is that we will repent from going our own way and believe in His way. May God grant us the gift of repentance – our only way out of the wilderness!

SCRIPTURES USED IN THIS CHAPTER

DEUTERONOMY 8:1-10 "Every commandment which I command you today you must be careful to observe, that you may live and multiply, and go in and possess the land of which the LORD swore to your fathers. And you shall remember that the LORD your God led you all the way these forty years in the wilderness, to humble you AND test you, to know what WAS in your heart, whether you would keep His commandments or not. So He humbled you, allowed you to hunger, and fed you with manna which you did not know nor did your fathers know, that He might make you know that man shall not live by bread alone; but man lives by every WORD that proceeds from the mouth of the LORD. Your garments did not wear out on you, nor did your foot swell these forty years. You should know in your heart that as a man chastens his son, SO the LORD your God chastens you.

"Therefore you shall keep the commandments of the LORD your God, to walk in His ways and to fear Him. For the LORD your God is bringing you into a good land, a land of brooks of water, of fountains and springs, that flow out of valleys and hills; a land of wheat and barley, of vines and fig trees and pomegranates, a land of olive oil and honey; a land in which you will eat bread without scarcity, in which you will lack nothing; a land whose stones ARE iron and out of whose hills you can dig copper. When you have eaten and are full, then you shall bless the LORD your God for the good land which He has given you.

NEHEMIAH 9:9-25 "You saw the affliction of our fathers in Egypt, And heard their cry by the Red Sea. You showed signs and wonders against Pharaoh, Against all his servants, And against all the people of his land. For You knew that they acted proudly against them. So You made a name for Yourself, as IT IS this day.

And You divided the sea before them, So that they went through the midst of the sea on the dry land; And their persecutors You threw into the deep, As a stone into the mighty waters.

Moreover You led them by day with a cloudy pillar, And by night with a pillar of fire, To give them light on the road Which they should travel.

"You came down also on Mount Sinai, And spoke with them from heaven, And gave them just ordinances and true laws, Good statutes and commandments. You made known to them Your holy Sabbath, And commanded them precepts, statutes and laws, By the hand of Moses Your servant.

You gave them bread from heaven for their hunger, And brought them water out of the rock for their thirst, And told them to go in to possess the land Which You had sworn to give them.

"But they and our fathers acted proudly, Hardened their necks, And did not heed Your commandments. They refused to obey, And they were not mindful of Your wonders That You did among them. But they hardened their necks, And in their rebellion They appointed a leader To return to their bondage. But You ARE God, Ready to pardon Gracious and merciful, Slow to anger, Abundant in kindness, And did not forsake them. "Even when they made a molded calf for themselves, And said, 'This IS your god That brought you up out of Egypt,' And worked great provocations, Yet in Your manifold mercies You did not forsake them in the wilderness.

The pillar of the cloud did not depart from them by day, To lead them on the road; Nor the pillar of fire by night, To show them light, And the way they should go.

You also gave Your good Spirit to instruct them, And did not withhold Your manna from their mouth, And gave them water for their thirst. Forty years You sustained them in the wilderness; They lacked nothing; Their clothes did not wear out And their feet did not swell. "Moreover You gave them kingdoms and nations, And divided them into districts. So they took possession of the land of Sihon, The land of the king of Heshbon, And the land of Og king of Bashan.

You also multiplied their children as the stars of heaven, And brought them into the land Which You had told their fathers To go in and possess. So the people went in And possessed the land; You subdued before them the inhabitants of the land, The Canaanites, And gave them into their hands, With their kings And the people of the land, That they might do with them as they wished. And they took strong cities and a rich land, And possessed houses full of all goods, Cisterns ALREADY dug, vineyards, olive groves, And fruit trees in abundance. So they ate and were filled and grew fat, And delighted themselves in Your great goodness.

CHAPTER FOURTEEN

MOSES' FINAL TEACHING

Scripture Text: Deuteronomy 9:1-6, 9, 18, 24, 27; 10:12, 13

Before the children of Israel go on to the twelfth step there are three other matters that the Lord wanted to deal with. **One** was that Moses was going to bring a clear understanding to the people about what God expected from them as they were in final preparations to go into the Promised Land. **Secondly,** Moses was teaching them what was expected of them after they got into the place of Promise. We will deal with both of these in this chapter. **Thirdly,** God was making a change in leadership. God always makes the chain of command clear. He was going to make a clear transition before the final step into the Land took place. We will deal with that in the next chapter.

First, let's deal with what Moses taught them about because this teaching applies to us today. We can gain great insight into our own journey with these teaching "points." In the last chapter we learned the **first teaching point that Moses taught was that God's agenda in the wilderness was threefold: 1) humble them, 2) test them, 3) teach them to live by God's word.**

The **second teaching point that Moses brought to the people was God's plan to provide the way for them to possess the Promise.** This teaching point covers what God's role would be in the victory over the enemies that currently resided in the Promised Land. In Deuteronomy 9:1-6 the plan is spelled out. First, Moses tells them forthrightly that where they are going, the nations are stronger and the people are bigger than they are! Also, the cities are very difficult if not impossible to overtake! This is not a very comforting teaching but it is important to bring life into perspective.

Whatever it is the Lord has promised us in life is beyond us. It's been said if we can do it on our own then it probably is not what God had intended. In life we always have this tension between us achieving everything we can with the talents and abilities that God has given us, and going beyond ourselves, so that the glory that comes to us will clearly belong to God. One of the greatest temptations in life is that after a successful venture, we have a tendency as people to forget the Lord's role in the achievement.

Moses goes on in this passage to tell them the solution to these humanly impossible things to overcome. He simply says that the Lord will go before you. Not only will His Presence go but that Presence will take on the form of a consuming fire to destroy the enemies right in front of your face – you will see it! Then you will drive them out quickly. In other words there will be no protracted fighting and you will not have to fear losses of life.

Interestingly, the Lord through the teaching of Moses, quickly adds here that He is not doing this because the children of Israel are better than the occupants of the Land. He is going to kill and drive them out because the present inhabitants are a wicked people. They are wicked in that they worship other gods. In fact, Moses teaches here that He is going to give them the Land because of His Promise to Abraham and not because of their righteousness – for they are still "stiff-necked." Moses then goes on to rehearse for them all the times in the forty years that they rebelled against and provoked God. It is always important for us to keep life in perspective from His viewpoint and not to even trust our own perceptions. We know we can never "earn" the Promises of God. Our works of righteousness are as filthy rags. We all fall short. We don't get what we deserve and we can thank the Lord that we don't. Because after all, we have all fallen short of what is required of us by God.

The **third teaching point** was to know what did God expect of the people? Expectations are a funny thing. Humanly we would look at the challenge of conquering the Promised Land; we could admit it is more than we could handle on our own. Then we would add up what it would take to win the war. In fact many would want to get a positive attitude and claim they are ready to win at any cost - do what you have to do – you can do it – and other various kinds of positive thinking strategies to inspire ourselves to try to accomplish the victory. But from God's perspective victory was not up in the air. He did not expect them to conquer the various enemies that would try to thwart their efforts to take over the Promised Land – He already assured victory. As usual what the Lord expected from the people had to do with their attitudes and condition of their hearts.

<u>Deuteronomy 10:12,13</u> *And now, Israel, what does the LORD your God require of you, but to **fear** the LORD your God, to **walk** in all His ways and to **love Him**, to **serve** the LORD your God with all your heart and with all your soul, AND to **keep***

the commandments of the LORD and His statutes which I command you today for your good?

It is clearly spelled out what the Lord expected of them. They were to do the following: **1)** fear the Lord, **2)** walk in His ways, **3)** love Him, **4)** serve the Lord thy God with all thy heart and with all thy soul, **5)** keep the commandments and statutes of the Lord.

God is much more interested in who we are rather than what we can do. Humanly we make decisions about people based on what we think they can accomplish. But since God has declared that all things are possible with God, then human ability is actually irrelevant. Human willingness to cooperate with God and believe in Him now takes precedence over human ability. He was not then, nor is He now, looking for people that are better than other people. He is looking for people that will believe that nothing is too difficult with God.

This teaching point goes to the motives of the heart. We are expected to fear the Lord. Doing so will then govern our actions accordingly. Our respect for Him will be so great that our behavior patterns will reflect our fear and respect for Him. On a human level we often feel like we can do some things because "no one is looking," or "I will not get caught." But with God, He is always looking and we will always get caught.

We are expected to walk in His ways. In **Isaiah 55:8-11**: *"For My thoughts ARE not your thoughts, Nor ARE your ways My ways," says the LORD. "For AS the heavens are higher than the earth, So are My ways higher than your ways,   And My thoughts than your thoughts. "For as the rain comes down, and the snow from heaven, And do not return there,   But water the earth, And make it bring forth and bud,   That it may give seed to the sower And   bread to the eater, So shall My word be that goes forth from My mouth; It shall not return to Me void,   But it shall accomplish what I please,   And it shall prosper IN THE THING for which I sent it.*

This passage tells us that His ways are higher than our ways. God always takes the high road in a matter. His ways reflect that the way things are done is more important than what is done. His ways reflect that why we do something is more important than what we do. We can actually do the right thing for the wrong reason and it is sin. It is very popular today to say, "What would Jesus do?" - as in this particular situation that I may be in? But the real question is why would Jesus do what He would do in this situation? We are expected to find why and how He would do what we are faced with and then do it for His reason and His way.

We are expected to love God. This expectation is born out of the principle of reciprocity. The Lord has been motivated to create us and work with us, and He sent His Son to die for us because He so loves us. His motivation is love, He is love, and the reason He does everything is out of love. Because He first loves us He expects us to receive that love and to respond to it by loving Him in return. In the New Testament Jesus was asked what is the most important commandment? Without hesitation He responded that, what sums up the commandments is, that "we are to love the Lord our God with all our heart and with all our soul and we are to love our neighbor as ourselves." Love is the glue that is to hold a Christian together. It is to be the motive behind every relationship both horizontal – with people – and vertical – with God.

We are expected to serve the Lord with everything we have and everything we are. When you serve someone or something you are placing yourself under them. This means you are humbling yourself and putting that person above you. This affects what we do because now we no longer use the criteria of what seems good to me is what it is that I want to do. We will do those things that we find are what seems good to the One we are serving. This service is to be done in harmony of the soul, which is the level of the mind and our thought process, as well as on the level of the heart. In other words, we are not doing something because it looks like we are doing well, but on the inside we are resenting it. No, what we are doing on the outside is born out of a heart to serve on the inside.

The **last aspect of this teaching point** in preparation for going into the Promised Land is that **we are expected to keep the commands of God**. He expects us to obey Him. He says later in scripture that obedience is greater than sacrifice. Jesus said He did not come to do away with the law but that He came to fulfill the law. This means that Jesus held to the highest standards of what the Father expected out of a man. One of the goals of Jesus as He emptied Himself of His Deity and came in like fashion as we are, was to fulfill all that was expected of Him. In fact, when He was on the cross, He declared it is finished! What was finished was that He did everything that the Father had expected of Him, right up to those last breaths He took on the cross.

Now **secondly**, after Moses brought this clear teaching about the expectations of God, he then goes into an outline of what the people should do after they got into the Promised Land. The Bible has several examples of the "final" words of a passing leader. The Bible often uses these words as prophetic. They always bring a perspective of someone that has both succeeded and failed in their own walk with God, and they have pearls of wisdom to give to the next generation. **Moses reminds them that the key to victory is to hear God's words and obey them.** Starting in Deuteronomy 11:26 and through Deuteronomy 30 Moses spells out what **God's agenda** is for them after they get into the Promised Land.

The **first thing** they were to do after they defeated the enemy was to destroy every place that idol worship was practiced. Every altar and image was to be destroyed, so that there was to be no evidence of their prior existence. God was not going to share their affections with another deity.

The **second thing** they were to do was to find where God wanted to establish a place of meeting. Moses' tabernacle in the wilderness was also called a place of meeting. God supplied the design of the tabernacle, down to the very detail. God orchestrated all the rules of use and the order and methods and who was eligible to do what in the worship that took place at the meeting. Moses was now informing them that God would also spell out where and how worship would take place in the Promised Land. (As a footnote here; it took the Children of Israel four hundred and sixty years to find the meeting place that God had wanted. David found it on Mt. Zion in the city of Jerusalem.)

Now these two things are not mutually exclusive. When we come to know Christ as our Savior we are to break with all other things that we have worshipped and served in our lives. We are to tear down every remembrance of these things in our life. Sometimes that means a change of friends or a change of places that we normally go to, or a change of things we do. At the same time He requires us to find that place to meet with Him that He chooses. Often we want to meet Him in the place we choose for ourselves. Again we must search for His view, how does He see what we should do and where we should go?

In addition, we must learn to spend a lot of meaningful time with our Lord. Often we think in terms of time spent. But it is more than clock time at a meeting that He is interested in. We have trouble grasping the significance of His purposes for meeting with us in the first place. The Lord requires of us not only our time but He wants our participation on the level of the heart. Our meetings are to have elements of interaction. They are to be exclusive expressions of love and devotion that take place at these meetings. We are to stay current in all of the expectations that He has for us. We are to worship Him and none other.

For our purposes here let's take a look at an outline of the remaining expectations that Moses left with the people, that they were to do after they possessed the Promised Land:

* Rules of worship – (Chapts.11 – 13)

* Rules of food -- (Chapt.14)

* Rules of debt -- (Chapt.15)

* Rules of Passover and the Feasts – (Chapt.16)

* Rules of law – (Chapt.16:8, 17)

* Rules of care of Priests – (Chapt.18)

* Rules of indictment – (Chapts.19.20)

* Rules of human relationships – (Chapts.21 – 26)

* Rules of tithing and first-fruits – (Chapt.26)

* Results of obeying or disobeying – (Chapts.26-28)

* Call to commitment and covenant – (Chapt.29)

* Choose life or death – (Chapt.30)

As we can see God has an order for our lives. It is quite detailed and covers all areas of life. Even so it is more than a behavior model for living. He has taken forty years in the wilderness to establish the nature of relationship that He planned for a people that He could call by His name. There is much that He wanted yet to do for them. He wanted to bless them and help them to multiply and be fruitful. He wanted the world to see the benefits that accrued to a people that would walk according to His principles for living. He intended to use the children of Israel as a testimony to the rest of the world of how wonderful it is to love and serve the living God.

The reason for this was so that the rest of the world would come to Him for Salvation and Deliverance. As much as God intended to pour out His love to them it was also to show the world how much the Lord loved all people just as much. These people were not chosen for their inherent superiority. They were chosen because of Abraham. We have been chosen because of Jesus. We have no inherent superiority over others. We have just been fortunate to recognize our need for Him, and have been blessed because we turned to Him.

Now God was trying to spell out for the children of Israel in great detail just how responsive He wanted them to be. And He told them that to the degree they would respond to His expectations, is the degree He would respond to them. It becomes our responsibility to know what He expects. We find it in His Word. He wants us to know His Word and obey it. The one thing God made very clear to them and for that matter to us as well is that if we leave Him to go and serve other gods, He will become angry and separate from us and will give us over to evil and to the curses of the law.

Without getting into the issues of eternal security, let us realize that our life with God is interactive and conditional. His promises always carry conditions. We have a tendency to major on the promises and not talk about the conditions that go with them. God's expectations on us are rarely taught. We often reduce them to a behavior model that leaves out the heart model.

These expectations are healthy for us. They will enable us to live for Him:

1) Fear the Lord

2) Walk in His ways

3) Love God

4) Serve the Lord

5) Keep His commandments

May we walk in the power of His Spirit that will enable us to live for Him on a new level of His expectations for us in this life?

SCRIPTURES USED IN THIS CHAPTER

DEUTERONOMY 9:1-18 "Hear, O Israel: You ARE to cross over the Jordan today, and go in to dispossess nations greater and mightier than yourself, cities great and fortified up to heaven, a people great and tall, the descendants of the Anakim, whom you know, and OF WHOM you heard IT SAID, 'Who can stand before the descendants of Anak?' Therefore understand today that the LORD your God IS He who goes over before you AS a consuming fire. He will destroy them and bring them down before you; so you shall drive them out and destroy them quickly, as the LORD has said to you.

"Do not think in your heart, after the LORD your God has cast them out before you, saying, 'Because of my righteousness the LORD has brought me in to possess this land'; but IT IS because of the wickedness of these nations THAT the LORD is driving them out from before you. IT IS not because of your righteousness or the uprightness of your heart THAT you go in to possess their land, but because of the wickedness of these nations THAT the LORD your God drives them out from before you, and that He may fulfill the word which the LORD swore to your fathers, to Abraham, Isaac, and Jacob. Therefore understand that the LORD your God is not giving you this good land to possess because of your righteousness, for you ARE a stiff-necked people.

"Remember! Do not forget how you provoked the LORD your God to wrath in the wilderness. From the day that you departed from the land of Egypt until you came to this place, you have been rebellious against the LORD. Also in Horeb you provoked the LORD to wrath, so that the LORD was angry ENOUGH with you to have destroyed you. When I went up into the mountain to receive the tablets of stone, the tablets of the covenant which the LORD made with you, then I stayed on the mountain forty days and forty nights. I neither ate bread nor drank water. Then the LORD delivered to me two tablets of stone written with the finger of God, and on them WERE all the words which the LORD had spoken to you on the mountain from the midst of the fire in the day of the assembly. And it came to pass, at the end of forty days and forty nights, THAT the LORD gave me the two tablets of stone, the tablets of the covenant.

"Then the LORD said to me, 'Arise, go down quickly from here, for your people whom you brought out of Egypt have acted corruptly; they have quickly turned aside from the way which I commanded them; they have made themselves a molded image.'

"Furthermore the LORD spoke to me, saying, 'I have seen this people, and indeed they are a stiff-necked people. Let Me alone, that I may destroy them and blot out their name from under heaven; and I will make of you a nation mightier and greater than they.'

"So I turned and came down from the mountain, and the mountain burned with fire; and the two tablets of the covenant WERE in my two hands. And I looked, and behold, you had sinned against the LORD your God—had made for yourselves a molded calf! You had turned aside quickly from the way which the LORD had commanded you. Then I took the two tablets and threw them out of my two hands and broke them before your eyes. And I fell down before the LORD, as at the first, forty days and forty nights; I neither ate bread nor drank water, because of all your sin which you committed in doing wickedly in the sight of the LORD, to provoke Him to anger.

DEUTERONOMY 9:22-29 "Also at Taberah and Massah and Kibroth Hattaavah you provoked the LORD to wrath. Likewise, when the LORD sent you from Kadesh Barnea, saying, 'Go up and possess the land which I have given you,' then you rebelled against the commandment of the LORD your God, and you did not believe Him nor obey His voice. You have been rebellious against the LORD from the day that I knew you.

"Thus I prostrated myself before the LORD; forty days and forty nights I kept prostrating myself, because the LORD had said He would destroy you. Therefore I prayed to the LORD, and said: 'O Lord GOD, do not destroy Your people and Your inheritance whom You have redeemed through Your greatness, whom You have brought out of Egypt with a mighty hand. Remember Your servants, Abraham, Isaac, and Jacob; do not look on the stubbornness of this people, or on their wickedness or their sin, lest the land from which You brought us should say, "Because the LORD was not able to bring them to the land which He promised them, and because He hated them, He has brought them out to kill them in the wilderness." Yet they ARE Your people and Your inheritance, whom You brought out by Your mighty power and by Your outstretched arm.'

CHAPTER FIFTEEN

LEADERSHIP TRANSITION

Scripture Text: Deuteronomy 31:1-8, 14, 15, 23; Numbers 20:7-13

In Deuteronomy 31: 1 Moses told the people that he was one hundred twenty years old and not as able to get around as he once did. Also he said that the Lord told him he was not allowed to go into the Promised Land. Although he quickly assured them that the Lord would go in with them and that Joshua would be their new leader.

If we go back to Numbers 20: 7-13 we will see the circumstances under which God made the decision that Moses would not be allowed to go in. It was at the time of Miriam's death, that the children of Israel were faced with another water shortage. The people as usual got upset and accusatory of both Moses and God, so Moses and Aaron went to God in prayer. God told Moses to take His rod, gather the people so that they can see you do this, and then I want you to **speak to the rock** and that is how you will give the people water to drink. So, Moses took the rod and gathered the congregation before the rock.

Now instead of making this a prayer meeting, Moses did something that many of us could identify with, but unfortunately it was a grave mistake. Moses got in front of the congregation and yelled at the people, "hear now you rebels; must we fetch you water out of this rock?" Then Moses lifted up his hand and with the rod he smote the rock two times, and the water came out abundantly. Remember God had told him to speak to the rock not hit it. Now in verse 12 the Lord spoke to Moses and Aaron immediately and said, "Because you did not believe me and you did not hold me special before the congregation, I will not let you go into the Promised Land."

This seems like a stiff penalty for a leader that we could justifiably argue was provoked into this fit of temper. After all, the people had failed on ten occasions to respond in faith to God and Moses failed only one time, why couldn't he just be forgiven and let's go on? Well, first of all it tells us that in 1 Corinthians 10: 4 that there was a Rock that followed the children in the wilderness and that the Rock was Christ Jesus.

The Bible clearly makes a point that this moment belonged to God and was not a moment for human leadership to put on a dramatic display. What God was after was bringing the people to a new dimension of understanding of His provision and at the same time of His character. This Rock was to be a type of Christ. That means that this Rock provided the water of life day by day for the people for the next forty years. This Rock was with them wherever they went. It was to be a constant reminder to the people of God's provision for His them. This Rock was to be a picture of God's promised Salvation. In the New Testament we come into a fuller revelation of the Rock - Christ Jesus. Jesus is the Rock of our Salvation. The Church is built upon the Rock - Christ Jesus. Jesus is the foundation of the Church. This was to be the introduction of that revelation and Moses failed in this vital moment in his role.

God also said that this represented a revelation of Moses' own place of unbelief. This was a serious charge. We could also say that Moses acted presumptuously, by striking that which the Lord held sacred. And Moses was not honoring God. He spoke to the people as if he were doing the fetching of water rather than obeying God and showing the people the Source. Now Moses did not lose his standing with God. He was still the man God used to lead the people. He still had historical prominence in the context of the history of this people. He still is the one that the angel Michael contended with the devil for his body, which Michael said belonged to God (Jude 9). But this act disqualified Moses from entering the Promised Land!

There was a man that the Lord was grooming in the wings. Joshua was the man that was always there for Moses. He was not perceived as the number two man per se, that was probably Aaron's place. But Joshua's faithfulness was beyond reproach. In fact Hebrew scholars place Joshua as getting the tabernacle, or meeting place, prepared on a daily basis. He probably rose each day at 3:30 a.m., and all by himself went to the tent to get things ready. Probably the only one watching him was God! He was a faithful servant to Moses. We would probably see him today as the man that carried Moses' bags for forty years and eleven months.

The number two man is perhaps the toughest place to serve in the ministry. You are close enough to the number one man to see all his foibles and mistakes. Often you can catch yourself saying, "Why would he ever do it that way? Or, I think that is a mistake, or the people won't like that." At the same time there can be one of two things happen with the people: **1)** they see the number two man as always number two and cannot imagine him being promoted, especially after such a long time. **2)** There are other people constantly telling him he should have been number one all along, and are constantly stirring him up to not wait on God for promotion. But Joshua remained steadfast and we find not one mention of disgruntlement, or any type of rebellion whatsoever. He was a faithful servant; he remained humble and never showed a sign of yearning for the top spot.

Moses declared that the Lord had chosen Joshua as the leader to take them into the Promised Land. In Deuteronomy 31:7,23 it says that Moses had called Joshua up in front of all the people and charged him to be strong and of good courage. Moses went on to encourage him that the Lord would be with him and the people each step from here on in and that Joshua was God's chosen man to cause them to inherit the Land. Moses was taken up to a place called Mt. Nebo, where he was given the privilege to look at the Promised Land. He looked at it from a distance and saw that it was a good place. Then he died, and was laid to rest in such a manner that no one could ever find his tomb. Undoubtedly, in the succeeding generations people would have sought out his tomb to somehow worship there. Yet he was buried in the land of Moab and the Lord never wanted them trying to lay claim to this land that had not been promised to them.

We are told in Numbers 27:15-23 the in-depth account of Moses requesting a successor to be chosen by God. God told him to take Joshua who had the "spirit" and lay hands on him. God told Moses to do this in front of the priests and the people. Moses was also to give him some of the honor that resided on Moses and to charge the people to be obedient to him. The people were told that when Joshua said go in that they were to go in. When Joshua said to go out they were to go out. A key for a leader chosen by God is that he will lead in a way that the people are to follow. You can't lead people that will only go where they want to, and people won't go if the leader won't tell them which way to go. The people are to interact with their human leader as well as their Heavenly Leader. This does not mean that they can tell either leader what to do but it means that they are to have relationship.

After personally living a life of never truly coming under authority until later in life, I can attest to some keys for coming to grips with God's ways that include learning how to live under authority. One truth that I came to was the realization that no one could "make" me come under authority. It was something I had to learn to give up on my own. In other words, what I learned was that I had to make a decision to place myself under authority. No one else could make me accountable, I had to learn to make myself accountable to others and especially to the Lord. Often this is something that the Lord has to work with us on for quite some time. This is especially true for those of us who didn't learn how to live such a way early on in life. It begins with our parents, and then teachers in school, and then military life, or college, or in the work force. Sooner or later you come to the realization that you have to serve somebody else besides yourself. It seems like the more you fight with those that the Lord has placed in authority over you the worse those He places over you seem to become. We must submit ourselves and willingly come under authority if we are to ever find in life the place that He has Promised us.

One of the weakest places the Church is suffering with is the lack of proper authority in the Church. In the western church many congregations are running the church and using the Pastor and staff to do things the way they want things done. This is not Biblical. Many churches struggle with proper church government models. In the Book of Acts we see the Apostolic Council. We see Deacons preaching, as well as Apostles and Prophets. We see that Apostles make decisions that affect a local area. We see the Council come into play when the decisions affect the entire Christian world.

It is important to see that the Lord did not draw an organization chart to spell out for the Church just what the flow of government is to always be. There is some latitude and obviously there is no perfect model. But at the same time we should see that there were giftings given to the church that include Apostles, Prophets, Evangelists, Pastors, and Teachers. There are also gifts of administrations, and gifts of helps to serve the local church body.

Regardless of the model used we must each find our place of meeting with God in the setting of a local church. And when we find that place we are to place ourselves under the authority that the Lord is honoring in that local assembly. If you don't believe that the Lord is honoring that local authority then maybe you should not join yourself to that place.

While we are searching for a local church we should do so with two key goals in mind: **1)** where does the Lord want my family and me to meet with Him? In other words, where can we be sure He wants us to be and not what "feels" most comfortable or exciting to us. **2)** Will I place myself under the authority of that local leadership? Am I willing to be accountable to the leadership? If not don't join. But we must keep seeking God's meeting place. The one He has picked out for our life. Remember He has a local church planned for us that will enable Him to work with us the most effective and productive way. Where He wants us will bring about the fulfillment of His promises for us in this life.

Back to the children of Israel now, the in between times are over. They always do come to an end. And now they are ready, after forty years, for the twelfth step. Let's remember that God has promised the victory. He has clearly spelled out His expectations. He has clearly spelled out and established His lines of communication and authority.

SCRIPTURES USED IN THIS CHAPTER

DEUTERONOMY 31:1-8 Then Moses went and spoke these words to all Israel. And he said to them: "I AM one hundred and twenty years old today. I can no longer go out and come in. Also the LORD has said to me, 'You shall not cross over this Jordan.' The LORD your God Himself crosses over before you; He will destroy these nations from before you, and you shall dispossess them. Joshua himself crosses over before you, just as the LORD has said. And the LORD will do to them as He did to Sihon and Og, the kings of the Amorites and their land, when He destroyed them. The LORD will give them over to you, that you may do to them according to every commandment which I have commanded you. Be strong and of good courage, do not fear nor be afraid of them; for the LORD your God, He IS the One who goes with you. He will not leave you nor forsake you."

Then Moses called Joshua and said to him in the sight of all Israel, "Be strong and of good courage, for you must go with this people to the land which the LORD has sworn to their fathers to give them, and you shall cause them to inherit it. And the LORD, He IS the One who goes before you. He will be with you, He will not leave you nor forsake you; do not fear nor be dismayed."

DEUTERONOMY 31:14, 15, 23 Then the LORD said to Moses, "Behold, the days approach when you must die; call Joshua, and present yourselves in the tabernacle of meeting, that I may inaugurate him."

So Moses and Joshua went and presented themselves in the tabernacle of meeting. Now the LORD appeared at the tabernacle in a pillar of cloud, and the pillar of cloud stood above the door of the tabernacle.

Then He inaugurated Joshua the son of Nun, and said, "Be strong and of good courage; for you shall bring the children of Israel into the land of which I swore to them, and I will be with you."

NUMBERS 20:7-13 Then the LORD spoke to Moses, saying, "Take the rod; you and your brother Aaron gather the congregation together. Speak to the rock before their eyes, and it will yield its water; thus you shall bring water for them out of the rock, and give drink to the congregation and their animals." So Moses took the rod from before the LORD as He commanded him.

And Moses and Aaron gathered the assembly together before the rock; and he said to them, "Hear now, you rebels! Must we bring water for you out of this rock?" Then Moses lifted his hand and struck the rock twice with his rod; and water came out abundantly, and the congregation and their animals drank.

Then the LORD spoke to Moses and Aaron, "Because you did not believe Me, to hallow Me in the eyes of the children of Israel, therefore you shall not bring this assembly into the land which I have given them."

This WAS the water of Meribah, because the children of Israel contended with the LORD, and He was hallowed among them.

NUMBERS 27:15-23 Then Moses spoke to the LORD, saying: "Let the LORD, the God of the spirits of all flesh, set a man over the congregation, who may go out before them and go in before them, who may lead them out and bring them in, that the congregation of the LORD may not be like sheep which have no shepherd."

And the LORD said to Moses: "Take Joshua the son of Nun with you, a man in whom IS the Spirit, and lay your hand on him; set him before Eleazar the priest and before all the congregation, and inaugurate him in their sight. And you shall give SOME of your authority to him, that all the congregation of the children of Israel may be obedient. He shall stand before Eleazar the priest, who shall inquire before the LORD for him by the judgment of the Urim. At his word they shall go out, and at his word they shall come in, he and all the children of Israel with him—all the congregation."

So Moses did as the LORD commanded him. He took Joshua and set him before Eleazar the priest and before all the congregation. And he laid his hands on him and inaugurated him, just as the LORD commanded by the hand of Moses.

CHAPTER SIXTEEN

STEP 12

FINALLY, THE PROMISE

SCRIPTURE TEXT: JOSHUA 1:1-18; 2:11,12,24; 3:1-17; 4:7,14,19; 5:1-15; 6:2

All the **whYs** in the road were leading up to this time. Every time circumstances came up before the people during their journey, which caused them to ask **whY** did this or **whY** did that happen, it was so that they could be prepared for such a time as this. We are today at that place that is the sum of our experiences and decisions that we have made along life's way. They needed to go through what they went through so that God could lead them into the fullness of the Promise that He had for them as a nation.

Let us review a couple facts that will help us to understand the ways of the Lord for our own lives. **First** of all, the timing was in the hands of the Lord. Once again He is the One who determines the timing of such events. Don't get ahead of God. A lot of well meaning people seem to get anxious sometimes and want to get going. But God waited for the forty years to be up, He also waited upon the death and mourning time for Moses to pass. It is also important that God's next man was installed into leadership. If there was ever a thing to be clearly established for a group of people on their journey with God, it is to verify that His hand is on someone and that person is set into place. Never compromise God's appointed leadership. Notice there was never a competition between Caleb and Joshua. The topic was never brought up. Caleb was able to keep his place in faith and confidence.

Now there were a couple of other things that the Lord wanted to take care of that are very important and that gives us insight into the "ways of the Lord."

The first thing the Lord does is give affirmation to His "new" leader in Joshua. In Joshua chapter one we find that God affirms Joshua with these words three times - "be strong and be of good courage." These are important building blocks in leadership. After all he had been the number two man for forty years and he did need to see himself differently than he had all these years.

Taking a new look at ourselves can be a challenging experience. It is a breeding ground for insecurity when someone who has yielded to another all his life is suddenly the point man, the center of decision making and activity. These words from God were creative words. They were intended to create in Joshua a new outlook on life. This is one of the exciting aspects about serving God and following Him. We do not need to be what we were. Our future is not limited by our past. Our future is limited only by His purposes for us and our faith in Him to accomplish them. "Be strong and of good courage," were words that went into the heart and mind of Joshua and immediately took root and began to grow into reality. The reason for this "sudden change" is that it probably was in the heart of Joshua for many years. He was a man that believed God and when God spoke Joshua knew it was true. When God spoke "it" Joshua immediately "acted on it." This comes from a heart that meditates on the Word of God.

God then also made these promises to Joshua in chapter one: **1)** every place you walk in this Land I will give it to you, **2)** no man will be able to stand before you all the days of your life, **3)** you will divide up the Land among the tribes, **4)** follow all the commands that I have given you and you will prosper, **5)** do not be afraid nor dismayed for I will be with you all the way. These promises of God were assuring and strengthening to Joshua and to the people.

Joshua 1:8 gives us in the midst of the chapter, an understanding of the promises of God with attached conditions. It says, *"This book of the law shall not depart out of thy mouth; but thou shalt meditate therein day and night, that thou mayest observe to do according to all that is written therein; for then thou shalt make thy way prosperous, and then thou shalt have good success."* We see there is a promise of prosperity with a condition that they will follow the commands of God as well as His directives for how He wants them to live. There has been much prosperity preaching done in America over the last forty years that has left out the conditions of obedience to God's Word and has left out the commitment required of thinking about God's Word "day and night."

Meditating on God's word takes time and effort. We must read the Word daily. We must search for the thought the Lord is conveying to us in the particular place we are reading. We must search for what that Word is talking about. We must find out not only what the Word is talking about in the context it is written in, but also, we must find the Holy Spirit application of that Word to our own present day situation. What part of that Word applies to my life today? Does my life line up with that Word? Does that Word call for change in my life? Does that Word tell me something new about the Living God? Can I see something new about Him that will help me live for Him?

The Bible says about itself that "the letter kills but the Spirit gives life." This means that I must read the Word with the help of the Holy Spirit. And with purpose I must allow Him to guide me into all truth of God's Word for my life. The Bible says that no Word is void of power; this means there is power to live and serve God in His Word. But you and I must dig it out, just like a miner going after precious jewels in the earth. Imagine if we got one thought from God each day out of His Word. That would be three hundred and sixty five God thoughts per year and ten years later that would be three thousand six hundred and fifty God thoughts to help us live effective and productive lives for Him. Oh how healthy we would be individually and as a Church if only we would meditate on His Word day and night. "Man shall not live by bread alone, but by every Word that comes from the mouth of the Father."

The next thing that was settled was a commitment on the part of the people to do what Joshua told them to do. In fact, the people went so far as to propose the idea of the death penalty to any rebels that would not do what Joshua told them to do. Maybe they were finally sick and tired of suffering for the rebellion of others and thought they would take matters in their own hands. Interestingly, the people also proclaimed to Joshua the affirming words that he heard from the Lord when they said to him, "be strong and of good courage."

Joshua sent in two spies to the Land to see what was before them. They came back believing that God was going to give them the Land because they had heard from Rahab the harlot that the people of Jericho had been trembling for forty years over the day the children of Israel would come to Jericho and overtake them. Isn't it interesting that even waiting for forty years the people of Jericho had no better plan than to build strong walls? There was no evidence that they came up with any weapon or strategy to fight against the people of God. Again the spies of forty years before could not "see" how the inhabitants looked at the children of Israel. They were too busy looking at the situation from their own point of view to consider another way. Anyway, all of the present generation was encouraged to go forward and to possess the Land.

The final preparations for Step Twelve were very significant. Joshua sent the priests to the front of the line and they were carrying the Ark of the

Covenant. In other words, the Presence of God was going ceremonially before them. It was springtime and they had to cross the Jordan River, which was swollen and overflowing its banks with the mountain runoffs of melting snow. This time no one was afraid or in a panic. The priests were instructed to go to the edge of the water and take a step. Then God did the miraculous and parted the Jordan and they again walked across the riverbed on dry ground like they had the Red Sea. Again God walled up the river flow and the people took stones out of the middle of the riverbed and made a memorial on the "other side" of the Jordan for a testimony to future generations. Each generation owes the next generation a memorial of the goodness of God in their lives.

God did something unusual for Joshua here. In Joshua 4:14 we are told that God magnified Joshua in the sight of all Israel and they feared him as they feared Moses for the rest of his life. The people had heard from God that Joshua was the leader but now they saw it. This is settling for both Joshua and the people. It would put a halt to the endless speculations over who should "really" be leading this group. God always chooses a man to be His spokesman. It always behooves us to find out who that is and then support them and get behind them and stay there.

Now before there was to be any showdown or confrontations with enemies of the Land, God wanted to do something very important as the final preparation for the people to possess the Land. We are learning that for them to possess the Land they needed to learn how to "receive" the Land. As previously stated, when someone gives you a gift you need to know where it is and how to open it. In order for the children of Israel to receive that which God was going to give to them they needed to renew themselves in a very important aspect of relationship with their God. They needed God to do something for them spiritually, in order for them to be in the condition to receive what He had planned for them. They needed a specific renewal in their hearts regarding their past and God was going to give it to them.

God told Joshua in Chapter Five verse two that Joshua was to circumcise all the men that were born in the wilderness for they had not been circumcised. Now this is profound and often a missing element in our present day relationship with our Lord.

First, let us remember that Moses had trouble with his own revelation of the value and importance of circumcision. If we will remember his wife had to throw the knife at him to circumcise his own sons. He did not circumcise his own sons even though he himself was circumcised. He did not do it to his own sons until he was on his way back to meet with the elders of Israel and to lead them out of Egypt. Then, Moses did not see to it that any of the males born in the wilderness were circumcised. But now the Lord was saying that they couldn't go in until they were circumcised. This was to be the final preparation for Step Twelve. Joshua and the people obeyed and after crossing the Jordan River and before taking on any of the enemy they were circumcised.

The Lord announced that on that day He was rolling away the "reproach" of Egypt. What makes this so profound was that from that day forward no one ever brought up the idea of going back to Egypt. There is a day when the past does lose all power over us in the present. It may take a while but the time comes for the past to be done away with. There is a strong Biblical principle that teaches us that we are to go forward and not look back. When we put our shoulder to the plow we are not to look back. Lot's wife was told not to look back – the concept being that there was a longing in her heart to be back there and not where God was leading them. This was the final healing for the children of Israel that the Lord saved for this moment.

What is in the power of circumcision? First of all circumcision began with Abraham. He was told that it was a "sign" of the covenant. This means that it was not the covenant itself but it was a sign to the person himself that he was in a relationship with the God Almighty and Creator in which God decreed that the person circumcised belonged to Him – and that God likewise was available to that person. For five hundred years this was a sign of belonging to God. But Moses came along and saw that there were problems with that sign.

In fact, in both Deuteronomy 10:16 and 30:5 Moses prophesied that the day would come when the Lord would circumcise the "foreskin" of their hearts. Moses saw that the "sign" was not a very good sign as practiced by the people up to that time. That while the people were circumcised in the flesh that they still had a major heart problem. He saw that they needed heart surgery and that this would one day become the true sign of covenant relationship. In one verse he said that they were "stiff-necked" and that they needed their heart circumcised. In the other verse, he said that when their heart was circumcised that they would then love God with all their heart and with all their soul.

For us in the New Testament we find that circumcision of the heart is a much-needed revelation for the Church. We can go to Church but that in and of itself is not a sign of the covenant. We must spiritually enter into relationship with the Lord and the New Testament reveals that "entering in" takes place in the waters of baptism. If we seek the Lord carefully in these scriptures we will see that in the waters of baptism an operation of God takes place in our heart.

During this operation (which is spiritual), the Holy Spirit surgically removes that tendency to go our own way. At the same time He cuts away those things in our heart that hinder us from loving God with all our heart and soul (see Romans 2:28, 29; and Romans 6; and Colossians 2:10-14).

What happened to the children of Israel was that God did this work in the heart as they were circumcised in the flesh. The people were now in new relational territory with God. They needed to be on new footing and new revelation with God in order to go in and possess all He had planned for them. When He says that, "Today have I rolled away the reproach of Egypt from off you." He is telling us something that is intended to help us in this day and age. Egypt was a shameful place for the people. It is a shame to be a slave. It hangs over your head for generations. We can look in our own nation and still see the shame that hangs over the black people of America.

There is a pain that seems to run in the blood of people that have been enslaved by another people. In the Church's attempt to racial reconciliation we have missed the significance of Gilgal. This is the place where God rolled away the reproach. What is needed is a spiritual operation by the Holy Spirit. Only God can restore the place of shame for the past. Only in Christ are we made new creatures. Every one of us for that matter has come out of Egypt. Every one of us has done shameful things. Every one of us carries a burden from the past that God will roll away from us if we will meet Him in our own "Gilgal."

We cannot come into the Promises of God until we cooperate with Him in the things He needs to accomplish in us, so that we might be eligible to receive that which He has promised. It is an important preparation by God in us, to "roll away the reproach" from us. As we pray we can ask the Lord where and how He will do that in each of our lives. This we know, it is tied up in God doing something in our heart – God cutting away the power of the past so that we will not live in resentment to what happened to us in the past, nor focused on the unresolved nature of the past.

In Joshua 5:11-15 we now come to the final hours before Step Twelve that now was over forty one years in coming. In these final hours Joshua went off by himself to be alone with God. He had no plan for the invasion! He knew the invasion was imminent but did not "see" how it was to be accomplished. As Joshua was praying he saw a Man with a sword drawn. Joshua asked the Man, "are you for us or are you against us?" The Man answered that He is the Captain of the Host. This opened Joshua's eyes to see that he was before the Lord Himself. He immediately humbled himself and lay at the feet of the Captain of the Host. Had this merely been an angel He would have not let

Joshua prostrate himself. But the Lord received Joshua in this manner and told him to take off his shoes for he was on Holy ground.

The Lord told Joshua to look at Jericho and see that it is completely locked up. No one is coming in or going out. He then said, "See, I have given into your hand Jericho, the king of Jericho, and the army of Jericho." How could Joshua "see" all of that? Well, Joshua was able to "see" things from God's point of view. From God's point of view it was a done deal. Joshua was able to believe God. Joshua believed the Land was Promised to them. Joshua believed that the Promise was going to be fulfilled now. Joshua was able to see beyond his own limitations and beyond the limitations of the people. Joshua was able to see into the realm of God where the impossible becomes possible. Joshua did not suffer with doubt. Doubt always brings with it suffering. The strategy of God was then told to Joshua. We know the story well. They marched in silence and faith for seven days and on the seventh day the walls came tumbling down!

There is a twelfth step for all of God's children. May you walk in faith along life's journey? May every wall in your life "come tumbling down?"

SCRIPTURES USED FOR THIS CHAPTER

JOSHUA 1:1-18 After the death of Moses the servant of the LORD, it came to pass that the LORD spoke to Joshua the son of Nun, Moses' assistant, saying: "Moses My servant is dead. Now therefore, arise, go over this Jordan, you and all this people, to the land which I am giving to them—the children of Israel. Every place that the sole of your foot will tread upon I have given you, as I said to Moses. From the wilderness and this Lebanon as far as the great river, the River Euphrates, all the land of the Hittites, and to the Great Sea toward the going down of the sun, shall be your territory. No man shall BE ABLE TO stand before you all the days of your life; as I was with Moses, SO I will be with you. I will not leave you nor forsake you. Be strong and of good courage, for to this people you shall divide as an inheritance the land which I swore to their fathers to give them. Only be strong and very courageous, that you may observe to do according to all the law which Moses My servant commanded you; do not turn from it to the right hand or to the left, that you may prosper wherever you go. This Book of the Law shall not depart from your mouth, but you shall meditate in it day and night, that you may observe to do according to all that is written in it. For then you will make your way prosperous, and then you will have good success. Have I not commanded you? Be strong and of good courage; do not be afraid, nor be dismayed, for the LORD your God IS with you wherever you go."

Then Joshua commanded the officers of the people, saying, "Pass through the camp and command the people, saying, 'Prepare provisions for yourselves, for within three days you will cross over this Jordan, to go in to possess the land which the LORD your God is giving you to possess.'"

And to the Reubenites, the Gadites, and half the tribe of Manasseh Joshua spoke, saying, "Remember the word which Moses the servant of the LORD commanded you, saying, 'The LORD your God is giving you rest and is giving you this land.' Your wives, your little ones, and your livestock shall remain in the land which Moses gave you on this side of the Jordan. But you shall pass before your brethren armed, all your mighty men of valor, and help them, until the LORD has given your brethren rest, as He GAVE you, and they also have taken possession of the land which the LORD your God is giving them. Then you shall return to the land of your possession and enjoy it, which Moses the LORD's servant gave you on this side of the Jordan toward the sunrise."

So they answered Joshua, saying, "All that you command us we will do, and wherever you send us we will go. Just as we heeded Moses in all things, so we will heed you. Only the LORD your God be with you, as He was with Moses. Whoever rebels against your command and does not heed your words, in all that you command him, shall be put to death. Only be strong and of good courage."

JOSHUA 2:9-13 and said to the men: "I know that the LORD has given you the land, that the terror of you has fallen on us, and that all the inhabitants of the land are fainthearted because of you. For we have heard how the LORD dried up the water of the Red Sea for you when you came out of Egypt, and what you did to the two kings of the Amorites who WERE on the other side of the Jordan, Sihon and Og, whom you utterly destroyed. And as soon as we heard THESE THINGS, our hearts melted; neither did there remain any more courage in anyone because of you, for the LORD your God, He IS God in heaven above and on earth beneath. Now therefore, I beg you, swear to me by the LORD, since I have shown you kindness, that you also will show kindness to my father's house, and give me a true token, and spare my father, my mother, my brothers, my sisters, and all that they have, and deliver our lives from death."

JOSHUA 2:23, 24 So the two men returned, descended from the mountain, and crossed over; and they came to Joshua the son of Nun, and told him all that had befallen them. And they said to Joshua, "Truly the LORD has delivered all the land into our hands, for indeed all the inhabitants of the country are fainthearted because of us."

JOSHUA 3:1-17 Then Joshua rose early in the morning; and they set out from Acacia Grove and came to the Jordan, he and all the children of Israel, and lodged there before they crossed over. So it was, after three days, that the officers went through the camp; and they commanded the people, saying, "When you see the ark of the covenant of the LORD your God, and the priests, the Levites, bearing it, then you shall set out from your place and go after it. Yet there shall be a space between you and it, about two thousand cubits by measure. Do not come near it, that you may know the way by which you must go, for you have not passed THIS way before."

And Joshua said to the people, "Sanctify yourselves, for tomorrow the LORD will do wonders among you." Then Joshua spoke to the priests, saying, "Take up the ark of the covenant and cross over before the people."

So they took up the ark of the covenant and went before the people.

And the LORD said to Joshua, "This day I will begin to exalt you in the sight of all Israel, that they may know that, as I was with Moses, SO I will be with you. You shall command the priests who bear the ark of the covenant, saying, 'When you have come to the edge of the water of the Jordan, you shall stand in the Jordan.'"

So Joshua said to the children of Israel, "Come here, and hear the words of the LORD your God." And Joshua said, "By this you shall know that the living God IS among you, and THAT He will without fail drive out from before you the Canaanites and the Hittites and the Hivites and the Perizzites and the Girgashites and the Amorites and the Jebusites: Behold, the ark of the covenant of the Lord of all the earth is crossing over before you into the Jordan. Now therefore, take for yourselves twelve men from the tribes of Israel, one man from every tribe. And it shall come to pass, as soon as the soles of the feet of the priests who bear the ark of the LORD, the Lord of all the earth, shall rest in the waters of the Jordan, THAT the waters of the Jordan shall be cut off, the waters that come down from upstream, and they shall stand as a heap."

So it was, when the people set out from their camp to cross over the Jordan, with the priests bearing the ark of the covenant before the people, and as those who bore the ark came to the Jordan, and the feet of the priests who bore the ark dipped in the edge of the water (for the Jordan overflows all its banks during the whole time of harvest), that the waters which came down from upstream stood STILL, AND rose in a heap very far away at Adam, the city that IS beside Zaretan. So the waters that went down into the Sea of the Arabah, the Salt Sea, failed, AND were cut off; and the people crossed over opposite Jericho. Then the priests who bore the ark of the covenant of the LORD stood firm on dry ground in the midst of the Jordan; and all Israel crossed over on dry ground, until all the people had crossed completely over the Jordan.

JOSHUA 4:14 On that day the LORD exalted Joshua in the sight of all Israel; and they feared him, as they had feared Moses, all the days of his life.

JOSHUA 5:1-15 So it was, when all the kings of the Amorites who WERE on the west side of the Jordan, and all the kings of the Canaanites who WERE by the sea, heard that the LORD had dried up the waters of the Jordan from before the children of Israel until we had crossed over, that their heart melted; and there was no spirit in them any longer because of the children of Israel.

At that time the LORD said to Joshua, "Make flint knives for yourself, and circumcise the sons of Israel again the second time." So Joshua made flint knives for himself, and circumcised the sons of Israel at the hill of the foreskins. And this IS the reason why Joshua circumcised them: All the people who came out of Egypt WHO WERE males, all the men of war, had died in the wilderness on the way, after they had come out of Egypt. For all the people who came out had been circumcised, but all the people born in the wilderness, on the way as they came out of Egypt, had not been circumcised. For the children of Israel walked forty years in the wilderness, till all the people WHO WERE men of war, who came out of Egypt, were consumed, because they did not obey the voice of the LORD—to whom the LORD swore that He would not show them the land which the LORD had sworn to their fathers that He would give us, "a land flowing with milk and honey." Then Joshua circumcised their sons WHOM He raised up in their place; for they were uncircumcised, because they had not been circumcised on the way.

So it was, when they had finished circumcising all the people, that they stayed in their places in the camp till they were healed. Then the LORD said to Joshua, "This day I have rolled away the reproach of Egypt from you." Therefore the name of the place is called Gilgal to this day.

Now the children of Israel camped in Gilgal, and kept the Passover on the fourteenth day of the month at twilight on the plains of Jericho. And they ate of the produce of the land on the day after the Passover, unleavened bread and parched grain, on the very same day. Then the manna ceased on the day after they had eaten the produce of the land; and the children of Israel no longer had manna, but they ate the food of the land of Canaan that year.

The Commander of the Army of the LORD

And it came to pass, when Joshua was by Jericho, that he lifted his eyes and looked, and behold, a Man stood opposite him with His sword drawn in His hand. And Joshua went to Him and said to Him, "ARE You for us or for our adversaries?"

So He said, "No, but AS Commander of the army of the LORD I have now come."

And Joshua fell on his face to the earth and worshiped, and said to Him, "What does my Lord say to His servant?"

Then the Commander of the LORD's army said to Joshua, "Take your sandal off your foot, for the place where you stand IS holy." And Joshua did so.

JOSHUA 6:1, 2 Now Jericho was securely shut up because of the children of Israel; none went out, and none came in. And the LORD said to Joshua: "See! I have given Jericho into your hand, its king, AND the mighty men of valor.

The circumcision of heart prophesied by Moses and picked up by Apostle Paul in the New Testament:

Deuteronomy 10:15-17 The LORD delighted only in your fathers, to love them; and He chose their descendants after them, you above all peoples, as *it is* this day. Therefore circumcise the foreskin of your heart, and be stiff-necked no longer. For the LORD your God *is* God of gods and Lord of lords, the great God, mighty and awesome, who shows no partiality nor takes a bribe.

Deuteronomy 30:6 And the LORD your God will circumcise your heart and the heart of your descendants, to love the LORD your God with all your heart and with all your soul, that you may live.

Romans 2:28, 29 For he is not a Jew who *is one* outwardly, nor *is* circumcision that which *is* outward in the flesh; but *he is* a Jew who *is one* inwardly; and circumcision *is that* of the heart, in the Spirit, not in the letter; whose praise *is* not from men but from God.

Colossians 2:11-14 In Him you were also circumcised with the circumcision made without hands, by putting off the body of the sins of the flesh, by the circumcision of Christ, buried with Him in baptism, in which you also were raised with *Him* through faith in the working of God, who raised Him from the dead. And you, being dead in your trespasses and the uncircumcision of your flesh, He has made alive together with Him, having forgiven you all trespasses, having wiped out the handwriting of requirements that was against us, which was contrary to us. And He has taken it out of the way, having nailed it to the cross.

EPILOGUE

The Bible often refers back to the experiences of the Great Exodus. Much can be gained by studying these scriptures to get into the Bible's interpretation of the events cited here in this book. The more we can understand what God was looking for in them during their journey the more we will understand what He is looking for in us. This will help us better learn how to respond to Him, and learn how to see things from His viewpoint. Below is a partial list of some of the more complete references to the journey recorded and interpreted in other parts of the Bible:

Nehemiah 9:23-26

Psalms 78:8-72

Psalms 19:7

Psalms 68:6

Psalms 71:17

Psalms 86:15

Psalms 103:7-17

Psalms 105:7-45

Psalms 106:4-48

Acts 7:2-45

Hebrews 3:2—19

Hebrews 9:1—9,19—23

Hebrews 11:23—31

DARYL T SANDERS

Daryl graduated from Ohio State with a degree in Marketing. He was the #1 draft choice of the Detroit Lions. Over the course of his multifaceted career Daryl worked for a Fortune 500 company becoming Exec. VP, he left to build a Cadillac dealership. Later he became a pastor and started a local church in Columbus, OH. There he took missionary trips all over the world but especially to Ukraine that he visited 13 times. He became an avid student of the Bible and has spoken to thousands of people both in America and abroad. He became a well known advocate for the poor and disadvantaged in central Ohio, working with urban and suburban churches to advance this cause. His books reflect his thoughtful views on the topics covered – not taking the obvious teachings prevailing in the Western Church culture, but challenging his readers to learn how to think about and read the Bible for themselves. Daryl's thrust of Bible interpretation is based on his assumption that our religion should be based on discovering what God wants from us rather than what can we get out of God.

OTHER BOOKS BY DARYL T SANDERS

Peter Finds Life The most controversial disciple, who discovered something about Jesus that the others missed. He learned to "tap into" Jesus more than any of the others and as a result was the clear leader in the church startup.

Peter Finds Power This book looks at every mention of Peter in the book of Acts. We see him be the first in every major expression of faith possible in the birthing of the early church. He preached the first sermon, healed the first sick person, he baptized new believers into the Holy Spirit, he was the first to preach to the gentiles, first to water baptize gentiles, he changed the paradigm of early believers that salvation was for all men and did not require a Jewish conversion to be saved. He was the first to testify in court, he was the first to be led by an angel out of prison; he was the first to raise the dead. We learn how Peter tapped into the power to accomplish these tasks and how we can tap into the same power.

Peter Finds Purpose In the Bible, 1 and 2 Peter were written by Peter some 30+ years after the resurrection of Jesus. They were written while Peter was in prison and about to die as Jesus had told him he would before the ascension. The books are powerful because they represent the number one ambassador and one of the key founders and builders of the church. In these two epistles Peter gives clear direction about what is important in life. Interestingly, he does not go back over any of his accomplishments but rather directs all that would read his words how they should live for God. He says in essence, it is not what you do for God but how you live for God that matters. He rehearses what are the key character qualities that lead to a productive life in Christ here on earth. He promises participation in the Divine nature of God if we will progressively walk in these character qualities.

God the Father This book discovers why, of all of the identities that God could have chosen to call Himself, that He called Himself Father! He could have been President, Dictator, Chief, General, and so forth. But He chose to identify Himself to us as ...Father. This gives us tremendous insight into His character, and how he desires to relate to us. It also helps us understand how He offers to care and provide for us and how we can learn to depend on Him and our relationship with Him.

The book goes on to uncover the specific functions of the Father as He fulfills his role.

Most people somehow think God is somewhere off around the North Star and that He is real busy. They don't want to bother Him with the trivial, but would rather save Him for the big stuff in their lives. This is a false view of God. He has chosen to make Himself available to all people all the time. He cares about each of us and LOVES EACH OF US. When each of us begin to understand that He is "my" heavenly Father, we can then begin to grasp His desire to be with us and involved with us at all times in all places.

This book will help each reader to discover just how available God is to each of us and what He offers to us as we walk on this earth during our life journey.

WHY? Questions along life's Journey This book gives us a unique insight into the two viewpoints of life that every person experiences as they live their life on earth. It takes the journey of Israel coming out of Egypt and going on their way to the Promised Land and all the **WHY'S** that happened to them along the way. **WHY** did we end up with a sea in front and the Pharaoh behind? **WHY** do we not have water already here for us to drink? **WHY** is there no meat? **WHY** is this trip so hard?

We all wonder why things happen to us along life's way. It is interesting to note that the letter Y shows a fork in the road. When we start at the bottom there are two ways to go at the top. By examining how the children of Israel handled their choices we can maybe get some insight on a better way for us to make better choices in our own lives.

Man in the Middle The God of Abraham, Isaac, and Jacob. Most of us know Abraham and know about Jacob, but very little known about Isaac. He was the bridge between the two and almost altered history.

Finding the Power to Heal Amazingly in Christian circles the topic of healing stirs as much controversy as it does in the secular world. Healing is mysterious for sure, as there is no proven single method whether by current medical science or by prayer to heal devastating sicknesses. But, healing is to be a part of the Christian experience and it is vital to discover how to tap into the power that is available to a believer in Christ Jesus.

The Bible gives us the keys to finding our healing. But it takes discovery to find out which keys will apply to us in any given situation. When those words in the Bible come alive in our heart we can find the faith it takes to receive our healing. We need to find what will trigger our faith to release the power in our lives.

The author, Daryl T Sanders, has prayed for thousands of healings over his Christian life in the past forty years. He has seen all kinds of healing from cancer to headaches, yet, as is true of all believers there were those he has prayed for that did not get healed. The author has reviewed most of the major healing examples in the Bible to help find which may stir the faith of the reader to be healed.

The book is a journey of faith and the reader is encouraged to read the book with an open mind and heart to see how they can find the power they need.

DAVID Chosen by God The name of David appears in the Bible more than the name of Jesus. In fact, Jesus used the name of David as a means of identification while He was on the earth. He claimed He was a part of his genealogy as proof that He was the foretold Messiah.

In the sixth-to-last verse of the Bible Jesus again identifies Himself as, "the root and offspring of David." When we consider how one man of all men ever born on earth could command such recognition, it demands an answer to why?

This book explores the life and times of David in the quest to answer this question. As we consider certain possibilities we can gain insight into what God is expecting from us. The book takes events as told in the Bible and adds some interpretive thoughts that might have been experienced by the historical figures. It starts out with David as a little shepherd boy who even before puberty displayed unusual courage in the face of danger.

The book takes the reader through David's life as the warrior of warriors, to the fugitive running from the king, to the victorious general, to king of Judah and then king of Israel, to worshipper, to architect, to husband and perhaps failed father that finally succeeds. We find David a renaissance man before the Renaissance.

His obvious failures seemed overshadowed by his incredible creativity to write music, make musical instruments, and choreograph singers and dancers into twice daily momentous worship services. He even designed the most expensive building ever built on earth.

With highs and lows in victory and defeat as David's life experience — Acts 13:22 says —"He raised up for them David as king, to whom also He gave testimony and said, 'I have found David the son of Jesse, a man after My own heart, who will do all My will.'"

The book seeks to discover the heart of the man and how he fulfilled the will of God on earth.

Made in the USA
Charleston, SC
13 October 2011